MICHAEL TEMPLE

English
Homework
Exercises

OXFORD

Preface

This set of worksheets aims to cover the basic English skills, and should also help towards exam preparation, at every level up to further education.

The generally accepted usages or "rules" of Standard English grammar, punctuation and spelling are seen as essential aids to clear communication, opening doors of opportunity for the student. Familiarity with these rules should help with all formal contexts like letter writing, and even job applications.

The sheets can be used by individual students to diagnose and remedy problems, or collectively in class and for homework. Each sheet is freestanding to allow focus on specific problems like the apostrophe or spelling rules. But the sections taken together also provide manageable and systematic courses on, for instance, sentence-building, word-choices or common errors.

The length of time needed for each double page should be equivalent to a lesson and a homework, the page of exercises requiring between 30 minutes and an hour. Answers where appropriate are provided at the back of the book.

Oxford University Press, Great Clarendon Street, Oxford OX2 6DP

Oxford New York
Athens Auckland Bangkok Bogota Bombay
Buenos Aires Calcutta Cape Town Dar es Salaam Delhi
Florence Hong Kong Istanbul Karachi
Kuala Lumpur Madras Madrid Melbourne
Mexico City Nairobi Paris Singapore
Taipei Tokyo Toronto Warsaw

and associated companies in
Berlin Ibadan

Oxford is a trade mark of Oxford University Press

Individual pages of this book may be reproduced by individual teachers for class use within the purchaser's institution. The material remains copyright under the Copyright, Designs and Patents Act, 1988, or in the case of reprographic reproduction in accordance with the terms of the licences issued by the Copyright Licensing Agency. No part of this publication may be reproduced for other purposes without prior permission of Oxford University Press. Enquiries concerning reproduction outside those terms and in other countries should be sent to the Rights Department, Oxford University Press, at the address above.

© Michael Temple 1997
First published 1997
Reprinted 1997
Reprinted in this format 1998
ISBN 0 19 831449 3

Designed and Typeset by Mike Brain

Artwork by Sue Heap

Printed in Great Britain by St Edmundsbury Press Ltd,
Bury St Edmunds, Suffolk

Contents

1	**Parts of speech**	
1.1	The naming of parts	4
1.2	Pronouns	6
1.3	Verb forms	8
1.4	Conjunctions	10

2	**Punctuation**	
2.1	Capital letters	12
2.2	Ending the sentence	14
2.3	Commas	16
2.4	Apostrophes	18
2.5	Inverted commas	20
2.6	Colons and semi-colons	22

3	**Spelling**	
3.1	Spelling strategies	24
3.2	Say as you spell	26
3.3	It's not always how it sounds	28
3.4	Word-building	30
3.5	Endings, or suffixes	32

4	**Sentence-building**	
4.1	What is a sentence?	34
4.2	Phrases	36
4.3	Problems with phrases	38
4.4	Clauses	40
4.5	Using clauses	42
4.6	Paragraphs	44

5	**Common errors**	
5.1	Singular and plural agreement	46
5.2	Mind your verbs	48
5.3	Comparatives and double negatives	50
5.4	All in a twist	52
5.5	Accident blackspots	54

6	**Vocabulary skills**	
6.1	Using a dictionary and thesaurus	56
6.2	Express yourself better	58
6.3	Using imagery	60
6.4	Polish your style	62

Answers		65
Index		71

© Michael Temple: Homework English

EXPLANATION
The naming of parts

All the words we use have different jobs to do. They belong to different parts of speech.

1 Noun:
a naming word which names a person, creature, thing or quality: *table   girl   dog   danger*

Nouns which name particular people or places are called proper nouns. These always start with a capital letter: *Julie   Tokyo   Wednesday   February*

2 Pronoun:
a word that stands instead of a noun: *I   he   she   it   they   us*

3 Adjective:
a word that tells us more about a noun or pronoun:
a *happy* face   He is *sad*.

4 Verb:
an action word, which tells us what happened: She *screamed*.   John *phoned*.   No one *answered*.

A verb can also be about being, becoming or feeling:
He *is* ill.   Sarah *became* quiet.   Luke *felt* gloomy.

5 Adverb:
a word that tells you more about the verb, about how the action was done:
She screamed *loudly*.   John phoned *frequently*.

It can also tell you more about an adjective or another adverb:
It was *extremely* cold.   She did *very* badly.

6 Preposition:
a word used in front of a noun or pronoun to make a phrase showing where, when or how something was done: The cat was *in* the tree.   We will go *after* breakfast.   The man *with* grey hair.

7 Conjunction:
a joining word which links words or groups of words: fish *and* chips   for better *or* worse
I went to the shops *because* we needed bread.   She sang well *although* she was ill.

8 Interjection:
a word of exclamation: *Oh!   Wow!   Great!*

9 Article:
the word 'the' is called the definite article and the words 'a/an' are called indefinite articles.

You can see eight parts of speech at work in this sentence:

Parts of speech 1.1

© Michael Temple: Homework English

EXERCISES

The naming of parts

1 Underline the adjectives in these three sentences.

(a) The quick brown fox jumps over the lazy dog.

(b) The orange cat chased the tiny timid mouse.

(c) All animals are equal.

2 Read these two sentences and then list the parts of speech.

She was a tall girl with blue eyes. Her hair hung loosely over her shoulders.

two verbs ....

four nouns ....

one adverb .... two adjectives ....

one pronoun .... two prepositions ....

3 Name the part of speech for each numbered word.

It^1 was^2 a bright^3 cold day^4 in April, and^5 the clocks were striking thirteen. Winston

Smith, his chin nuzzled into^6 his breast in an^7 effort^8 to escape the vile^9 wind, slipped^{10}

quickly^{11} through the glass^{12} doors of Victory Mansions. (George Orwell)

1 .... 2 .... 3 ....

4 .... 5 .... 6 ....

7 .... 8 .... 9 ....

10 .... 11 .... 12 ....

4 Fill in the blanks and put the part of speech in the brackets.

(a) Italy is in the .... of Europe. (............................)

(b) Germany's football .... has been very successful. (............................)

(c) Paris is a/an .... city. (............................)

5 In these sentences the word 'round' is four different parts of speech. Write what each one is.

(a) Circles are round. (............................)

(b) Let's play a round of golf. (............................)

(c) The supermarket is only round (............................) the corner.

(d) You'll need to brake before you round (............................) the bend.

6 Underline all the conjunctions in this sentence.

She enjoyed fish and chips but didn't like mushy peas because they looked green and sickly.

7 Name the parts of speech of the numbered words.

Twas brillig and the slithy^1 toves^2

Did gyre^3 and gimble^4 in^5 the wabe^6.

1 .... 2 .... 3 ....

4 .... 5 .... 6 ....

© Michael Temple: Homework English

Parts of speech 1.1

EXPLANATION

Pronouns

1 Subject and object

These pronouns *I   he   she   we   they* are in the **subject** form. They do the action:
I beat Victor. *We* beat their team.

Subject   Object

These pronouns *me   him   her   us   them* are in the **object** form. The action is done to them:
Victor beat *me*. Their team beat *us*.

These pronouns *you   it* stay the same when subject or object:
You beat me. I beat *you*.

TAKE CARE! Peter and *I* went to the game. NOT Peter and me ...

They invited Sue and *me*. NOT They invited Sue and I.

The test is to take the proper name away, and see if the sentence still sounds right.
Also, note that the proper name always comes first and the pronoun after.

2 Pronouns after prepositions

When a pronoun comes after a preposition, for example, 'for', 'from' 'between', use the object form:
The birthday card was *from us*. He arrived at the party *after me*.

TAKE CARE! Take care when there are two words joined by 'and' or 'or':
for Anne and *me*   *between him* and *me*   *from them* or *us*

3 Relative pronouns

These are *who   which   that*. They relate (are linked) to a noun and are used instead of it:
I met a girl *who* had a pretty smile.
This is the pen *which* I always use.
PE is the subject *that* I dislike the most.

Use *who* for a person; *which* for a thing; *that* for either a person or a thing.

4 Common confusions

- Don't use pronouns vaguely. Who or what are you talking about?
  Don't say: *They* should do something about *it*.
  Say e.g.: The council should do something about homelessness.
- Decide if you want to talk about one or more things, and be consistent. Say either: *Cars* are very useful but *they* cause pollution or *The car* is very useful but *it* causes pollution.
- Be careful about using the pronoun 'one'. It can easily sound pompous. If you do use it don't use 'you' as well.
- In standard English write: *We* humans treat animals badly, even if in speech you might use the idiom *Us* humans, which is the object form.

Parts of speech 1.2

EXERCISES

Pronouns

1 Choose the right pronoun for each space.

(a) My brother and (me/I) .... both like 'Star Trek'.

(b) Between you and (me/I) .... it's all lies.

(c) I suggest you and (we/us) .... join forces.

(d) I'm only doing this for you and (she/her) ....

(e) It appears that Susan and (he/him) .... were working together.

2 Rewrite where necessary in standard English.

(a) Him and me are great friends.

....

(b) Tom and her have been going out together.

....

(c) Somehow you and he will just have to cope.

....

(d) That's all from Zeinab and me.

....

(e) Us poor devils never have any luck.

....

(f) Are there any letters for David and I?

....

3 Correct these sentences.

(a) One must speak politely and mind your manners.

....

(b) The rose is a hardy plant and they grow in most soils.

....

(c) Cars have many advantages, the main one being that you don't have to wait for it as you do for a bus.

....

....

(d) The reader reads on because they want to know what happens.

....

4 Correct the words in italics.

(a) He is the sort of person *which* I can trust.

(b) *Her* and *me* like to go surfing.

(c) If *one has* a car you tend to use *them* just for short trips.

(d) Thank you for inviting my sister and *I* to the party.

© Michael Temple: Homework English

7

Parts of speech 1.2

EXPLANATION
Verb forms

Verbs are action words:
He *steered* the boat.   She *screamed*.
A verb can also be about being, feeling or becoming: She *was/felt/became* ill.

1 Verb tenses

The **tense** of a verb tells us if the action:

happened in the **past**:  They won the war.
(did win, have won, had won)

is happening now, in the **present**:  They win the war.
(are winning)

will happen in the **future**:  They will win the war.
(will be winning, will have won)

In the brackets you can see a number of small words, such as: *did, have, had, are, will, be*. These are called **auxiliary** verbs. They help to make up the verb tenses.

2 Active and passive

Active verb – the subject does the action:
Dad (subject) *cooked* (active verb) an enormous meal.

Passive verb – the action is done to the subject:
The enormous meal (subject) *was cooked* (passive verb) by Dad.

Active verbs are more personal: You shouldn't smoke.

Passive verbs sound more official and formal: Customers are requested not to smoke.

3 Transitive and intransitive

A verb is **transitive** when it has an object after it. The object is the person or thing the action is done to:
She (subject) *burst* (verb) *the balloon* (object).

An **intransitive** verb has no object after it:
The bubble (subject) *burst* (verb).

4 Infinitive

Usually the word 'to' appears before the **infinitive**:
I like *to read*.
She does not know how *to cook* pastry.

5 Participles

All verbs have present and past **participles**.
The **present participle** is formed by adding 'ing' to the root of the verb: eat – *eating*; read – *reading*. The **past participle** is usually formed by adding 'ed' to the root of the word: work – *worked*; stop – *stopped*.

You can join participles with other words to make **participial phrases**.
Stopping suddenly, the player bent in pain.

Parts of speech 1.3   © Michael Temple: Homework English

EXERCISES

Verb forms

1 Choose the right word to fill in the blanks so that all the verbs are either in the present or in the past tense.

It (was/is) .... a moonlit night. The trees (throw/threw) .... shadows

across the garden. The owls (were/are) .... hooting . Badgers (started/are starting)

.... to pad across the lawn. Hedgehogs (are shuffling/shuffled) ....

over the patio. Inside the house the family (slept/sleep) .... on unawares.

2 Rewrite these sentences using the passive form of the verbs.

e.g. Everyone must obey the law. The law must be obeyed (by everyone). (Notice that you can leave out the person/thing doing the action.)

(a) Teachers teach English throughout the world.

....

(b) People grow grapes all over Europe.

....

(c) Burglars broke into the house.

....

3 Are the verbs as used in this passage transitive or intransitive?

(Transitive verbs have an object.) Put 'T' after the transitive ones and 'I' after the intransitive.

We had (_) a good time at camp. We swam (_), climbed (_) rocks, walked (_), laughed (_) a lot, and

ate (_) masses of food and sang (_) songs round the fire. Some people cried (_) when they left (_).

4 Replace the words in italics with the infinitive form.

e.g. Seeing is believing. To see is to believe.

(a) The driver swerved *so that he could avoid* the pedestrian

     (...).

(b) He liked *eating* (.............................) while she liked *drinking* (.............................).

5 These sentences start with participial phrases. Complete the sentences by adding a subject and verb.

e.g. Seeing the bus coming, the man (subject) ran (verb) across the road.

(a) Not noticing the black ice, ...

(b) Worried about his health, the ....

(c) Finding no one at home, ...

(d) Swerving recklessly, the ....

(e) Knocked down in the first round, the ....

© Michael Temple: Homework English

Parts of speech 1.3

EXPLANATION

Conjunctions

Conjunctions are words which join other words or groups of words e.g. because, if, although.

1 Stuck in a rut

Read this paragraph:

She awoke at six. She got out of bed. She went downstairs. She made a cup of tea. She got dressed. She had breakfast. She left for school.

The writer is 'stuck in a rut' using short sentences each with the same pattern. It sounds jerky and monotonous.

One way to improve this is to use **conjunctions** to join ideas:
When she woke at six, she got out of bed *and* went downstairs. She made a cup of tea, *then* got dressed. *Before* going to school she had some breakfast.

2 Rabbiting on

Conjunctions are useful but some of them are used too often. Read these two extracts aloud:

The bus didn't leave till midday so all morning we just lay around watching videos and then I packed my bags to go to Leyburn and then we stopped off at a shop so we could get some bait so we could go fishing.

Before I read this book I didn't think this sort of thing went on and I was horrified when I read the book and found out that people were getting killed and nobody was doing anything about it.

As you can hear, the writer keeps tagging bits on by using 'and' and 'so'. The result in each case is a rambling sentence. The same can happen if you use 'then' and 'also' too much.

3 Some solutions

- Give words like 'so', 'and', 'then' and 'also' a well-earned rest. Try doing without them for a while.
- Break up long rambling sentences into shorter sentences but be careful you don't end up 'stuck in a rut'.
- Try starting each new sentence in a different way.
- Try using conjunctions such as 'although', 'because', 'so that' and 'in order to' to make links between your ideas.
- Try using participial phrases like 'after stopping …', 'having finished …', etc.
- Read what you have written aloud and listen to it. Be prepared to re-write it if it sounds awkward or unclear.

EXERCISES

Conjunctions

Write answers on a separate sheet.

1 Rewrite this passage without using 'and'. Change the sentence construction and punctuation as you wish but keep all the information.

Yesterday I went to the wild-life park and saw the monkeys and the zebras and the lions and I had lunch and afterwards I had a ride on the camel and it was bumpy and I looked at a few more animals and went home.

2 Rewrite this without using 'then'.

I woke early and then got out of bed, then washed, and then I ate my breakfast, then set off for school and then met some friends.

3 Rewrite this without using 'so'.

It was raining so we decided to go to town for the day and take the rabbits to my grandma who gave us some money so we went and spent it in town.

4 Rewrite this, avoiding 'also'.

If a pregnant mother smokes the child can be small. Also if the father smokes his sperm can be abnormal. Also non-smokers have little risk of getting lung cancer.

5 Make two clear sentences out of these five, avoiding 'so' and 'then'.

The burglar climbed hastily out of the window. The burglar was terrified he'd be caught. The burglar didn't notice the water-butt. The burglar got stuck in the water-butt. The burglar was caught by a passing policeman.

6 Expand these notes into fluent sentences. Vary the length and pattern of your sentences and avoid 'then' and 'so'. Try not to use 'and' more than once.

girl went to night club – proud of new ring – worth £500 – ring loose on her finger – ring fell off – not noticed till next day – girl heart-broken – loss reported to police – girl returned to night club – saw something glinting on the ground – her ring – undamaged

7 Rewrite this fluently in two or three sentences. Don't use 'and' more than once and avoid 'then'.

I awoke in darkness. I was in great pain. I was tied up. I heard the roaring of water. I heard thunder. I also heard sailors shouting. The whole world seemed to turn upside down. The result was I was violently sick.

© Michael Temple: Homework English

Parts of speech 1.4

EXPLANATION
Capital letters

Capital letters for the start of all sentences:
> All sentences start with a capital letter.

A capital letter for all days and months:
> Monday, Thursday, January, September

Proper nouns or names of particular people, places and things have capital letters:
> John Smith, Edinburgh, Easter

Initials of names and groups as well as most words made from initials have capital letters:
> M.L.Bloggs, BBC, NATO (Note that full stops are often omitted now.)

Titles of all kinds (e.g. books, films, newspapers) take capital letters. If the title has several words in it, the first and all main words have capitals. (The same applies to headlines.):
> Animal Farm, The Wizard of Oz, the Daily Mail

Adjectives from proper nouns have capital letters:
> English, French, Victorian

Lines of verse usually have a capital letter at the start of each new line:
> Tiger, tiger, burning bright
> In the forests of the night...

Speech starts with a capital letter:
> He said, "Don't be late."

Remember too:
- 'I' always has a capital letter:
  I am the great I and I always have a capital I.
- A capital is also used in letters for Dear ... and Yours ... .

Punctuation 2.1

© Michael Temple: Homework English

EXERCISES
Capital letters

1 Write in capital letters where needed in these sentences.
(a) dave asked, "did you watch wolverhampton wanderers play manchester united in the f.a. cup?"
(b) the narrowest part of the english channel lies between the french port of calais and the english towns of dover and folkestone.
(c) i've just read 'animal farm' by the english writer george orwell and an american novel called 'of mice and men' by john steinbeck.
(d) the teacher said, "i don't much like the phrase 'mother nature', do you?"
(e) dr jones has the sign 'a.jones m.d.' on his surgery door.
(f) it wasn't clear whether joe potsky was a c.i.a. or a k.g.b. agent.

2 Write in capital letters where they are needed in the following.
(a) my name is gemma. i was born under the sign of gemini and i've just read my horoscope in the 'daily wail'. it says that thursday is going to be my lucky day. perhaps i'll buy a national lottery ticket then.
(b) "what's the capital of australia, jim?"
"sydney, isn't it?" said george.
"i reckon it's melbourne," said jo.
at this point julie piped up, "well, you're all wrong. it's canberra."

(c) my friend said, "my favourite songs are 'i will always love you' by whitney houston and 'redemption song' by bob marley."
i replied, "yeah, but i prefer 'a hard day's night' by the beatles."
(d) dear parents,
this term's christmas production is 'west side story' by leonard bernstein, a musical about rival gangs of puerto-ricans in new york. it takes place in the shakespeare theatre from tuesday december 17 to saturday december 21.

EXPLANATION
Ending the sentence

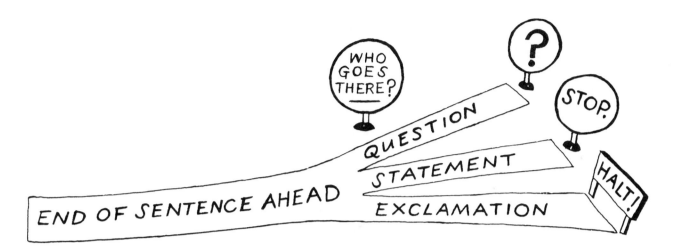

Sentences end with a full stop, question mark or exclamation mark (but not with a comma).

Here's how to check whether you've written a sentence and where it ends:
- Read it to yourself.
- Ask yourself if it makes complete sense.
- Check the part which follows in the same way.

1 Full stop
The full stop marks the end of **statements**, **commands** and **replies**:
I know how to use a full stop. (statement)
Stop. (command)
Of course I do. (reply to a question)

2 The question mark
This is used for direct questions:
Where are you going?

 Do not use a question mark if the question is reported: He asked her where she was going.

3 The exclamation mark
The exclamation mark is used for exclamations of shock, amazement or strong emotion:
Wow! Amazing! Rubbish!

4 Abbreviations
The full stop is also used after abbreviations, especially when the word is cut after its first letters, rather than contracted to include its last letter:
Co. (shortened form of Company)
but Dr (a contraction)
Rev. (shortened form of Reverend)
It is also used for some special abbreviations:
i.e. (= that is), e.g. (= for example), etc. (= and the rest).

Punctuation 2.2 © Michael Temple: Homework English

EXERCISES

Ending the sentence

1 Put extra large full stops and capital letters in these.

(a) Sam woke he noticed a dramatic drop in temperature it was 50 below freezing he felt his nose it didn't seem to be there any more

(b) to find where a sentence ends read it aloud to yourself you should then find where the statement ends each sentence can make sense on its own

(c) on Tuesday I went to my friend's house it was brilliant he had a fantastic car that he'd bought at an auction it was an ex-police car and was in excellent condition

(d) Nick's hand was shaky he reeled in slowly he felt sick because he'd lost a big fish

(e) when the people came to where the dragon lay, stretched out huge on the ground, the sight dismayed them they didn't dare approach or touch it some ran away some warned their friends not to go near the creature in case it had any life left in its body they explained that it might still be able to breathe fire over them others thought the dragon might have little dragons in its womb one person even claimed that the dragon's eyes were moving

2 Find the sentence ends in these. Put large full stops and capitals.

(a) it was raining the rain dripped from the trees water stood in the pools on the gravel path
(Ernest Hemingway)

(b) Kino deftly slipped his knife into the edge of the shell through the knife he could feel the muscle tighten hard he worked the blade lever-wise and the closing muscle parted and the shell fell apart the lip-like flesh writhed up and then subsided Kino lifted the flesh, and there it was, the great pearl, perfect as the moon (John Steinbeck)

3 Decide whether to use a full stop, question mark or exclamation mark in the bracketed spaces.

Help ( ) I'm sinking ( ) Can't anyone hear me ( )
I wonder what he's doing ( )
Tell me, please, why you did it ( )
Who he was nobody seemed to know ( )
Why are you so puzzled ( )

EXPLANATION

Commas

Commas are useful, but they can NEVER end a sentence.

Here are some uses of the comma:

1 Items in a list
They bought apples, pears, plums, cherries and raspberries.
He got up, dressed, ate his breakfast and rushed out of the house.
(Usually there is no comma before 'and'.)

2 Extra bits in sentences
- Ends of sentences:
  The comma looks like a tadpole, doesn't it? It's a useful punctuation mark, I reckon.
- Interjections and asides:
  Well, now you're talking. Yes, I certainly am.
- Shows the person(s) spoken to:
  Take a break, mate, when you feel like it. Hi, Steve.
- Adverbs used for emphasis or to link with previous sentence:
  Fortunately, she had a spare key.

3 Separating speech from the rest of the sentence
"Great idea," he said, to which she replied, "No, it isn't." "I hoped," he said, "you'd be impressed."

4 Making the meaning clear
After swerving round a corner that was very tight, the cyclist crashed to the ground.

5 In letters
Dear ...., and Yours faithfully, (or sincerely,) but you don't always find commas in addresses in business letters.

6 Extra information or comments
Libby, last year's prize-winner, hoped she would win again.
The lottery, as everyone knows, has been hugely popular.
You always need two commas in these cases.

Sometimes writers use brackets or double dashes:
Brackets are for small inserts (such as dates or page numbers) and to separate whole sentences.
(This sentence is an example.)

Double dashes emphasise an insert:
This sentence – and it's the last one on this page – contains double dashes.

Punctuation 2.3   © Michael Temple: Homework English

EXERCISES

Commas

1 Put commas where needed.
(a) For breakfast he had chips peas kippers pasta and cornflakes.
(b) I came I saw I conquered.
(c) Giggs the United striker scored the winner.
(d) "Friends Romans countrymen lend me your ears" shouted Mark Antony.
(e) Well you've done it now haven't you Steve?
(f) Does your Dad know you're here Kevin?
(g) The film is as anyone can see full of humour horror ghosts battles and murders.
(h) Abraham Lincoln President of the United States was assassinated by an actor.
(i) "I've no idea" she said "what you're talking about."

2 Insert commas where needed.

(a)
> Dear Jo
> We had a great day at Shellsea on Saturday playing cricket on the beach swimming in the sea and having a barbecue. The next day however was a real disaster just about everything going wrong. As it was raining hard in the morning we drove into the country getting lost and not finding anywhere for lunch. Finally and worst of all my brother was sick in the car. Well that's life I suppose. Can't wait to see you Pam.
>
> Jo
> St Hung St
> Slatone
> Howle
> PI7 PQ

(b) Oscar Wilde when he was asked what work he'd done in the morning said "I spent it putting in a comma." When asked what he'd done in the afternoon he replied "I spent it taking the comma out."

3 Put brackets or double dashes in these.
(a) Nothing at all tent, table, chairs or buckets could be left unguarded.
(b) Citrus fruits oranges, lemons and limes are very good for you.
(c) Last summer it was late August I climbed Ben Nevis.

4 Insert or take out commas in these sentences to change their meanings.
(a) Did you call Alex?
(b) Mrs Davis, the teacher, is late.

EXPLANATION

Apostrophes

1 Omission or contraction

Apostrophes show where there's an **omission** (letters have been missed out), or **contraction** (where a word has been shortened).

When we shorten words, the apostrophe shows where the letter(s) has been left out:

I'm = I am
doesn't = does not
they're = they are
can't = can not
won't = will not
shan't = shall not
it's = it is (or it has)

2 Who is the owner?

The apostrophe also shows us who is the **owner** of something.

- If the owner is singular (= just one), put an apostrophe and then an 's':
  Tom's cat (= belonging to Tom)
  the cat's whiskers (= the whiskers belonging to the cat)

- If the owner is plural (= more than one) and ends in 's', put an apostrophe after the 's':
  a cats' home (= a home for cats)
  the three ladies' cats (= the cats belonging to the three ladies)

- If the plural does not end in 's', put an apostrophe and then an 's':
  children's games (= games of the children); women's hats

 Do not use an apostrophe:

- after plurals that are not owners: The greengrocer sells apples and pears (*not* apple's and pear's).
- with these words: his, hers, ours, yours, theirs
- with its, when this means belonging to it:
  It's (= it is) only too obvious that it's (= it has) lost its (= belonging to it) tail.

3 Some special owners

- For phrases and joint owners put the apostrophe in the last word:
  The Leader of the Opposition's wife; William and Mary's house
- For names which end in 's' and which have more than one syllable, like Moses, Jesus, Archimedes, put just an apostrophe after the name. If the name has one syllable put an apostrophe and an 's':
  James's; Jones's.

Punctuation 2.4

© Michael Temple: Homework English

EXERCISES

Apostrophes

1 Rewrite these, using apostrophes to show the owners, e.g. the skin of the baby = the baby's skin.

(a) the paw of the monkey ....

(b) the paws of the monkeys ....

(c) the games belonging to the children ....

(d) a holiday lasting a week ....

(e) the exhausts of the lorries ....

(f) the votes of the people ....

(g) a speech by the chairman of the Water Board

....

(h) the shop belonging to the baker ....

(i) the wife of the Prime Minister ....

(j) for the sake of Jesus ....

2 Write the contracted forms as alternatives in the spaces.

I do not (...........................) see how we are (...........................) going to get a team for

tomorrow's match. Gill cannot (...........................) play, Sue has (...........................) got an

Achilles' heel injury and will not (...........................) be fit for weeks and Anne has

(...........................) got to go for a job interview. It is (...........................) sickening, is it not

(...........................)? And they are (...........................) all key players, are they not

(...........................)? I would have (...........................) asked Betty but no one has

(...........................) seen her for ages and there is (...........................) nobody else I can think of.

Let us (...........................) face it, it does not (...........................) look as if we have

(...........................) a chance of fielding a full side.

3 Cross out or add apostrophes as necessary.
(a) For sale: video's, computers', radios at bargain price's
(b) Theres no place like home. Too many cooks' spoil the broth.
(c) Whos that? Whats' that? How's that? Wheres that hammer?
(d) Its either her's or your's or maybe it's Sams youngest brothers.
(e) Did'nt you know the supermarket is now selling mens jumpers, childrens shoes and ladies coat's?
(f) The cars bumpers been smashed but it's drivers not hurt.
(g) Dont you know what youre doing by now?

© Michael Temple: Homework English

Punctuation 2.4

EXPLANATION

Inverted commas

Inverted commas, or quotation/speech marks, are used for: dialogue, quotations, titles, extra emphasis.

1 Punctuating speech or conversation

Like the bubble in a cartoon, **inverted commas/speech marks** wrap round the speech and any punctuation that belongs to it.

Here are three models:

- He said, "Do you know how to punctuate speech?"

  comma to break off   *capital letter to start speech*
  punctuation inside speech marks

- "We are working on it," they replied.

  comma to break off, then speech marks
  small letter as sentence isn't over

- "You seem," he said, "to have grasped it now. Well done."

  small letter   *comma to break off*
  small letter to continue speech
  close speech marks only when speech has finished

Apart from this, all you need to remember is:

- a new paragraph every time the speaker changes
- no speech marks if the speech is reported:
  He said (that) he would see us later.

2 Quotations

'Go to work on an egg' was a famous advert.
Oscar Wilde described fox hunters as 'the unspeakable in full pursuit of the uneatable'.

3 Titles

Put titles of books, films, TV shows, plays, houses, ships, newspapers and magazines in inverted commas:
'Animal Farm'; '2001 Space Odyssey'; 'Coronation Street'; 'The Sun'; 'H.M.S. Victory'

4 Using single or double inverted commas

You can use which you like, but if you need to use quotation marks within dialogue, be careful to make the two lots different:

"I enjoyed 'Jurassic Park'," she said. (Look carefully at the punctuation just before the word 'she'.)

In this book we've used double quotes for speech, and single for everything else.

Punctuation 2.5

© Michael Temple: Homework English

EXERCISES

Inverted commas

1 Rewrite these, punctuating where necessary.

(a) I'm sick as a parrot says sacked soccer boss.

....

(b) Pop star says I just want to be left alone.

....

(c) I want to be the country's ambassador says Princess Di.

....

(d) Bank robber admits he's no angel.

....

2 Punctuate and paragraph these.

(a) Jane asked her friends what's your favourite soap I like Eastenders replied Kate because it's full of real-life situations maybe said Gareth but don't you ever get bored with it? Coronation Street is much more realistic and it has some vivid characters Jane answered yes but I prefer Neighbours. It's much more modern and relaxed, and I love the last line of the signature tune: Good neighbours become good friends.

....

....

....

....

....

....

....

....

(b) I don't know what you're doing Alex said Simon but it isnt the proper homework, is it? I think I've learnt how to use the full stop, the comma and the semi-colon replied Alex. You ought to have studied inverted commas as well Simon pointed out.

....

....

....

....

....

....

© Michael Temple: Homework English

Punctuation 2.5

EXPLANATION
Colons and semi-colons

1 The colon

The colon tells you something is coming, such as **a list**, **spoken words**, **a quotation** or **an explanation**.

To succeed you need: will-power, your wits about you, some luck, plenty of stamina, and a little help from your friends.
He quoted Martin Luther King's famous speech: "I have a dream."
She won the music prize: she played the drums very well.

2 The semi-colon

- The semi-colon links **equal statements**.

  I am the semi-colon; I link equal statements.
  John is my brother; but Anne is my sister.
  They were poor; but they were honest.
  United we stand; divided we fall.

- Semi-colons link **short statements**:

  It was sunny; the sky was blue; the birds were singing.

  Here the semi-colon is being used instead of a full stop. You can do this especially if the statements are linked; remember that the statement that follows starts with a small letter.

- Semi-colons link **phrases in a list** especially if each item contains several words and commas:

  For the camping expedition you should bring: a tent, preferably lightweight; a back-pack containing extra clothing, cooking utensils and toiletries; string; matches; waterproofs.

3 Single dashes and hyphens

- Use a single dash if you want a dramatic pause:
  Go for it – the big dash!
  There could only be one result – defeat.

- The hyphen makes joined up words like tie-ups, partners-in-crime, brothers-in-law, a half-eaten biscuit.

4 Three dots

These show missing sections inside a passage or a tailing off at the end of a passage.
And finally ...

Punctuation 2.6 © Michael Temple: Homework English

EXERCISES
Colons and semi-colons

1 Put colons and semi-colons in these sentences.
(a) For this recipe you will need the following ingredients three eggs, preferably free-range two ripe, plum tomatoes a small onion and pepper and salt.

(b) Bring these items to the exam two pens, one black and one red a highlighter a pencil and a rubber.

2 Put colons in these.
(a) Hamlet's famous speech begins "To be or not to be …"
(b) Andy had a good job at the factory his father was head of the firm.
(c) I want to emphasise this we all support the proposal.

3 Put five semi-colons in this.
It was mid-October the sun was shining there was a feel of rain in the air. I was wearing my light blue suit it was the one I wore on my last case. I wasn't exactly looking for trouble even so, trouble had a way of finding me. I entered the room. It was empty not a mouse was stirring.

4 Put colons or semi-colons in these.
(a) Reading is an education in itself it helps you acquire a wide vocabulary.
(b) We will guard the tent you can gather some firewood.
(c) The past is a foreign country they do things differently there.
(d) The weather was threatening dark storm clouds were gathering gusts of violent wind rattled the window panes a touch of ice in the air made the flesh shiver.

5 Put a dash in each of these.
(a) We need new laws laws to protect the citizen.
(b) United win again by a whisker.
(c) Last year he climbed Ben Nevis but that's another story.

6 Decide where to put hyphens in this.
She is in full time employment, being fully trained, computer literate and hard working.

EXPLANATION

Spelling strategies

Always check your spelling, whenever you have doubts.
(Remember: a spellcheck can't teach you to spell!)

1   Have a learning system

This method will help you spell the common words you need most or keep getting wrong.
Then keep a list of the words you find most troublesome.

- **Look** at the word, preferably in a dictionary.
- **Say** it slowly, stressing any silent or slurred letters.
- **Write** it down letter by letter and underline the tricky part(s): sep_a_rate
- **Cover** the word and memorise it.
- **Write** it down without looking.
- **Check** letter by letter.

2   Use a dictionary

A dictionary does not only tell you how to spell a word. You can also use it to:

- check the **pronunciation**, as this may affect the spelling, especially when you add '-ing' or '-ed'
- note other words in the same **family**: medicine and medical
- note the **origin** of the word, as this can make sense of the spelling:
  biscuit is from bis = twice + cuit = cooked.

3   Invent memory aids

For the really troublesome words you will need to use or invent a memory aid:
Stick *gum* in an ar*gum*ent.
Friend has the *e* at the end.
You *gain* with a bar*gain*.
There are one *collar* and two *socks* in ne*cess*ary.
Catch the *bus* in *bus*iness.

4   Respect the rules and heed the hints

- Is it 'ie' or 'ei'? There's a rule to learn for this (see 3.2).
- Sounding a word out will sometimes help you to spell it: interested, business, vegetable, medicine, twelfth, February.
- Watch for tricky beginnings: *dis*appear, *add*ress, *occ*asion, *occ*ur, *unn*ecessary,
- Watch out for unexpected letters in the middle of words: excitement, meanness, skilful, loneliness, religious.
- To decide whether you need to double the consonant, pronounce the word first, to see where the stress falls: be*gin* – beginning; *happ*en – happening.
- Adverbs – double 'l' or not? Usually you add '-ly' to the end of the adjective: immediately, sincerely, completely but also faithfully, really, accidentally.
- Look out for odd ends: sentence, excellent, elegant, expense, visitor.
- Some words you just have to learn: embarrass, exaggerate, favourite, disastrous, conjure, argument, quarter, thorough, tragedy, accommodation, etc.

Spelling 3.1

© Michael Temple: Homework English

EXERCISES

Spelling strategies

1 **Use a learning system to learn ten words, choosing those you need most but keep misspelling.**

2 **Invent a memory aid for the two common words you have most trouble spelling.**
(But don't choose any of those in the Explanation notes.)

3 **Underline the slurred 'uh' or 'er' sounds or the lost letters in each of these words:**

| twelfth | elegant | visitor |
| interested | ridiculous | decision |

4 **Underline the 'difficult' bit(s) in each of these words.**

separate	surprise	occasionally	immediately
humorous	definite	beginning	exaggerate
tragedy	embarrass		

5 **Say these words and then underline the part that is stressed.**

| occur | benefit | refer | offer |

6 **Break these adverbs up so that you can see how they have been formed:**
e.g. simply = simple – drop 'e' add 'y'.

really ....

completely ....

carefully ....

immediately ....

probably ....

7 **Find 16 words, each of more than three letters, in this wordsearch and write them down carefully.**
(There are no diagonals.)

B	Y	Y	L	L	A	C	I	S	A	B
O	L	L	A	D	I	A	G	E	E	E
D	N	E	I	Q	F	R	O	P	V	G
I	N	T	D	S	R	G	N	A	I	I
S	A	A	D	U	E	U	P	R	E	N
S	R	I	I	O	I	M	E	A	C	N
O	P	D	A	I	G	E	Z	T	E	I
R	F	E	P	C	H	N	I	E	R	N
C	O	M	M	I	T	T	E	D	O	G
A	H	M	G	V	H	F	S	T	O	F
E	S	I	R	P	R	U	S	E	C	W

25

© Michael Temple: Homework English

Spelling 3.1

EXPLANATION
Say as you spell

Pronouncing words can often help you spell them.

1 'ie' or 'ei'?
Say the word. Is there a long 'eee' sound?
- If the word has an 'eee' sound put 'ie': bel*ie*ve, f*ie*ld.
- If the 'eee' comes after 'c' put 'ei': c*ei*ling, rec*ei*ve.
- If there is no 'eee' sound put 'ei': w*ei*gh, h*ei*ght.
(But see: friend, weird, seize)

2 Short and long vowels
The vowels are *a e i o u*. In some short words the vowel sound is **short**: hop; tap. In some words the vowel sounds are **long**: hope; tape. (The silent 'e' tells you a vowel sound is long.)

See what happens when we add endings that begin with a vowel (like '-ing' and '-ed').

Base word	Rule	Result
words with short vowels	double the last letter	
hop		hopping, hopped
bat		batting, batted
words with long vowels	drop the silent 'e'	
hope		hoping, hoped
excite		exciting, excited

3 Adding vowel endings to longer words
What happens when we add vowel endings such as '-ing', '-ed', '-able', '-er' to longer words that end in one vowel and one consonant, such as 'happen' and 'occur'? Say the word to see where the **stress** falls:

Base word	Rule	Result
words with the stress at	double consonant	occurring,
the *end*	to keep the vowel	occurred
occur refer	'short'	referring, referred
words with stress *not*	don't double	
at the end	the consonant	happening, happened
happen offer		offering, offered
words that end in 'l'	double the consonant	
travel		travelling, traveller
quarrel		quarrelled

4 Adding endings beginning with consonants
Just add endings like '-ness', '-ful', '-ment' to the end of the word: sad – sad*ness*, care – care*less*, hope – hope*ful*, excite – excite*ment*, prefer – prefer*ment*. But note: argue – argument.

5 'C' and 'g': the soft and the hard
- To keep a 'c' or 'g' soft (like a 's' or 'j' sound), before '-able' or '-ous', the silent 'e' stays: noti*ce*able, manage – mana*ge*able, courage – coura*ge*ous.
- To keep a 'c' hard (a 'k' sound) before '-ing'/'-ed'/'-er', insert a 'k': panic – pani*ck*ed, picnic – picni*ck*ing.

Spelling 3.2

© Michael Temple: Homework English

EXERCISES

Say as you spell

1 Apply the 'ie/ei' rule.

rec___ve   gr___f   n___ghbours   pr___st   l___sure   n___ce   bel___f

dec___ve   rel___ve   conc___ted

2 Apply the rule for adding vowel endings to short and long vowels. (The silent 'e' tells you the vowel is long.)

(a) Add '-ing' to each of these (e.g. hop – hopping):

plan ....   bar ....

stare ....   star ....

slope ....   recite ....

(b) Add '-ed' to each of these (e.g. hop – hopped):

wrap ....   describe ....

pine ....   skim ....

pin ....   excite ....

3 Apply the rule for doubling consonants when adding vowel endings. Say the words first.

(a) Add '-ing' to each of these (e.g. confer – conferring):

refer ....   orbit ....

omit ....   occur ....

quarrel ....   offer ....

(b) Add '-ed' to each of these (e.g. confer – conferred):

suffer ....   offer ....

expel ....   target ....

cancel ....   admit ....

4 Apply the soft and hard 'c' and 'g' guidelines to fill in the gaps in these.

outrag___us   notic___ble   servic___ble   mimic___d

5 Use the scrambled letters to make up the word which has the meaning shown: e.g. VBEEELI – believe.

HIFMSCEI = naughtiness	M ....
EZISE = grab	S ....
DRRREEEPF = liked more	P ....
VEEERCI = accept	R ....
INGROFE = abroad	F ....
IIEOURLGS = holy	R ....
GRINE = rule of a king	R ....
OIEMMTTCD = carried out	C ....
DERRUCCO = happened	O ....
EEECIMNTX = thrill	E ....

© Michael Temple: Homework English   Spelling 3.2

EXPLANATION

It's not always how it sounds

Pronouncing a word will not always help you to spell it. This is because spelling and pronunciation have changed over the centuries and because we have absorbed so many words from other languages.

1 Same sounds ~ different spellings

Often the same sounds will have different spellings:

'f' in family   'ph' in physical
'k' in kettle   'c' in calendar   'ch' in character
'j' in jealous   'ge' in general
'g' in gardener   'gh' in ghastly   'gu' in guardian
's' in sentence   'sc' in scene   'c' in ceiling
'n' in noticeable   'gn' in gnarled   'kn' in knot
'r' in ridiculous   'rh' in rhythm.

Remember these when you look words up in the dictionary.

2 Silent letters

Remember these: 'b' as in climb, comb and doubt; 'n' as in autumn, solemn, column; 'p' as in cupboard (for cups), receipt (reception); 'g' in reign and foreign.

3 Lost letters

A good way is to stress the lost letter e.g. int*e*rested, twel*f*th, s*ur*prise.

4 Uh! (or 'er')

Many vowels end up being pronounced with a neutral 'uh' or 'er' sound. Try saying these words, overdoing the letters in italics: des*cri*ption; cert*ai*n; mem*o*rable; ad*mi*ration.

5 Long words

Break them down into parts e.g.

sec – re – tary   con – tem – por – ary
un – nec – ess – ary   Wed – nes – day.

6 Whoops!

Check whether you are saying the word correctly:
Are you saying 'mischievious' instead of 'mis*chie*vous'; 'reckernise' instead of 're*cog*nise'?

7 Is it 'c' or 's'?

I advi*s*e you to take my advi*c*e.
The verb (advi*s*e, practi*s*e,) has 's'.
The noun (some advi*c*e, a practi*c*e, a licen*c*e, a prophe*cy*) has 'c'.

8 Do I write one word or more?

● These are each one word: *tomorrow, cannot, whereas, although*
● These are more than one word:

in fact   *in front*   *in between*   *a lot of*
lots of   *as well*   *no one* (but nobody)
in spite of   *all right*

(If you can't remember these, try taking a breath between each word.)

Spelling 3.3   © Michael Temple: Homework English

EXERCISES

It's not always how it sounds

1   Write these out correctly.

(If in doubt, use your dictionary.)

seenik ....   telefoan ....

nollej ....   fizziks ....

2   Put in the missing letters.

su__prise   tom__stone   gover__ment   choc__late

unint__rested   qua__ter   Feb__uary   We__nesday

3   Say these words and underline the part or parts that are slurred or usually pronounced with an 'uh' sound:

description   decision   visitor
bargain   mathematician   certainly

4   Break these words up into parts to make them easier to spell,

e.g. secretary = sec - ret - ary.

particularly   = ...

similarly   = ...

unnecessarily   = ...

extraordinary   = ...

5   Pronounce these words carefully. If in doubt look them up in the dictionary. Underline the part of the word which might be misspelt.

athletics   mischievous   recognise
century   hundred   asphalt

6   Underline the right 's' or 'c' word.

(a)   I must licence/license my car and buy the dog a licence/license.

(b)   There will be a singing practice/practise. Soloists will practice/practise next week.

7   How many words? Write this out with correct spacing.

infrontofalotofcannotalthoughinspiteoflotsofaswelltomorrow
whereaseverywhereinfactnooneinbetween

....

....

....

....

© Michael Temple: Homework English   29   Spelling 3.3

EXPLANATION
Word-building

Many words are made up of blocks or parts called
- **base words/roots**
- **prefixes** (bits put in front)
- **suffixes** (endings).

(prefix)	(root)	(suffix)
re	build	ing
inter	rupt	ion

1 Roots

As words come in 'families', knowing a few 'roots' will help you spell several common words:
fini (= end, limit) is in de*fini*te, in*fini*te, *fini*sh
sci (= know) is in con*sci*ous, *sci*ence, con*sci*entious
para (= get or set) is in se*para*te (= set apart), pre*para*tion.

2 Prefixes

- Knowing the common prefixes will also help you with spelling (and understanding meaning):
  de (= down) as in *de*scend (climb down)
  dis (not/apart) in *dis*approve.

3 Adding prefixes

- Normally, you just add the prefix to the base word or root:
  dis + appear = *dis*appear; *dis* + appoint = *dis*appoint;
  dis + service = *dis*service; *un* + natural = *un*natural.

- But sometimes prefixes change to double the first letter of the base word or root:
  'ad' (= towards) can change to *at*tract; *ap*point; *an*nounce
  'con' (with) can change to *cor*respond and *col*lect
  'in' (not) can change to *il*legal, *im*mortal and *ir*regular
  'ob' (in the way) can change to *oc*cur and *op*pose
  'sub' (under) can change to *suf*fer and *sup*plant.
  The words 'all' and 'well', when used as prefixes, drop one 'l': *al*mighty, *wel*come.

4 Adding consonant suffixes

Consonant endings such as '-ful', '-ness', '-ment', '-less' are normally just added to the root:
hope + *ful* = hope*ful*; stubborn + *ness* = stubborn*ness*; excite + *ment* = excite*ment*;
care + *less* = care*less*.

5 Changing 'y' to 'i'

If the root ends in a consonant + 'y', change the 'y' to 'i' when you add the ending:
happ*y* – happ*i*ness, happ*i*ly   marr*y* – marr*i*es
But not before '-ing': marr*ying*, carr*ying*, worr*ying*.
But if there is a vowel before the 'y' just add the suffix: survey – surv*eys*, surv*eyed*, surv*eying*.

Spelling 3.4

EXERCISES

Word-building

1 Look in a dictionary for a word starting with each of these common prefixes. Find out its meaning too. Write the word and its meaning on a separate sheet of paper.

ante = before	anti = against	bi/bis = two, twice
circum = around	contra/contro = against	dis = part, not
extra = beyond, outside	fore = before, in front	hyper = over, too much
hypo = under	in = into or not	inter = among, between
intro = within	mis = not, wrongly	ob = in the way
per = through	peri = around	post = after
pre = before, in front	pro = onwards	se = apart
sub = under	super = over	sur = on, over
tele = far	trans = across	un = not

2 Add 'dis-', 'mis-', or 'un-' to these words to make different meanings, e.g. spell – misspell.

appoint ....   necessary ....   understanding ....

natural ....   similar ....   laid ....

3 Study the section of the Explanation on prefixes that adapt. Then form the words in this list, e.g. ad + tract (draw) = attract.

ad + range   ....   ad + nounce   ....

ad + prove   ....   ad + breviate   ....

con + rect   ....   con + memorate   ....

con + mit   ....   con + rupt   ....

in + legible   ....   in + mature   ....

in + relevant   ....   in + resistible   ....

ob + position   ....   ob + cur   ....

sub + pose   ....   sub + fix   ....

4 Add consonant endings to these words.

(a) -ment to these: manage ....   excite ....

advertise ....   achieve ....

(b) -ness to these: mean ....   keen ....

happy ....   lively ....

(c) -ful to these: care ....   success ....

pity ....   beauty ....

(d) add -less to these: hope ....   clue ....

care ....   pity ....

5 Add '-ing' and '-ed' to these.

carry ....   journey ....   marry ....

pity ....   envy ....   reply ....

satisfy ....

© Michael Temple: Homework English

31

Spelling 3.4

EXPLANATION

Endings, or suffixes

1 Adverbs

- Normally you can just add '-ly':

  extreme – extreme*ly*   careful – careful*ly*
  final – final*ly*   real – real*ly*
  actual – actual*ly*   definite – definite*ly*
  faithful – faithful*ly*   accidental – accidental*ly*

  (Note: '-ful' becomes '-fully' and '-al' becomes '-ally'.)

- There are some exceptions to this rule:

  Words ending in '-ic' form adverbs in '-ically':
  basic – bas*ically*   terrific – terrif*ically* (but publi*cly*)
  Words ending in 'y' change to 'i' before the '-ly':
  happy – happ*ily*   temporary – temporar*ily*
  Words ending in '-ble' and '-ple' drop the 'e':
  simple – simp*ly*   probable – probab*ly*
  Also: true – tru*ly*   due – du*ly*
  whole – whol*ly*   full – ful*ly*

2 Plurals

- Usually, simply add 's' (or 'es' after 's' sounds - s, ss, sh, ch, x, z):

  apple – apple*s*   bench – bench*es*
  gas – gas*es*   class – class*es*

- If the word ends in a consonant and then a 'y' change the 'y' to 'ies':
  lady – lad*ies*   lorry – lorr*ies*

- If there is a vowel before the 'y', just add 's':
  valley – valley*s*   Wednesday – Wednesday*s*

- Add 's' to most words ending in 'o' but note the common exceptions:
  tomato – tomato*es*   potato – potato*es*
  hero – hero*es*   echo – echo*es*

- Words ending in 'f' or 'fe' often change to 'ves': knife – kni*ves*, thief – thie*ves*, wife – wi*ves*,
  leaf – lea*ves*.
  (But see: roofs, chiefs)

- Some words have odd plurals:
  child – *children*   man – *men*   woman – *women*

3 Some odd endings

- '-er': garde*ner*; charac*ter*; '-or': doc*tor*, profes*sor*, solici*tor*, visi*tor*; '-ar': gramm*ar*, burgl*ar*,
  calend*ar*, simil*ar*, particul*ar*
- '-ary': imagin*ary*, second*ary*, diction*ary*; '-ory': lavat*ory*, observat*ory*; '-ery': cemet*ery*;
  '-ury': cent*ury*, lux*ury*
- '-tion' (say 'shun'): educa*tion*, satisfac*tion*; '-sion': persua*sion*; '-ssion': posse*ssion*, commi*ssion*;
  '-cian': musi*cian*, politi*cian*
- '-ous' (often added to a full word): danger – danger*ous*
  '-eous' (often to keep the 'g' soft): gorg*eous*, outrag*eous*
  '-ious' (often to keep the 'c'/'g soft): reli*gious*, vi*cious*
- '-ant/-ance': eleg*ant*, relev*ant*; '-ent/-ence': differ*ent*, magnific*ent*, sent*ence*
- '-able/-ible': prob*able*, avail*able*; but poss*ible*, vis*ible*

Spelling 3.5   © Michael Temple: Homework English

EXERCISES

Endings, or suffixes

1 Make these into adverbs ending in '-ly' e.g. extreme – extremely

occasional ....   beautiful ....

skilful ....   improbable ....

humble ....   tragic ....

immediate ....   lucky ....

actual ....   automatic ....

merry ....   separate ....

successful ....   horrible ....

2 Put these into the plural form e.g. box – boxes, child – children

roof ....   half ....

potato ....   glass ....

video ....   jockey ....

lorry ....   valley ....

factory ....   battery ....

sandwich ....   pony ....

3 Put the correct endings on these.

auth__r	famili__r	furth__r	second__ry
compuls__ry	cemet__ry	lux__ry	politi__n
posses__n	profes__n	relig__us	courag__us
differ__nt	relev__nt	sent__nce	vis__ble

4 Fill in the blanks.

faithfu__y	sincer__y	peculi__r	emper__r
notic__ble	scientific__y	chang__ble	irresist__ble
respons__ble	visit__r		

5 Fill in the blanks.

(a) doct__r's surg__ry; solicit__r's secret__ry;

laborat__ry techni____n; garden__r; survey__r;

profess__r; schol__r; music__n; volunt__ry worker; veh__c__ maint__n__ce supervis__r

(b) respons__ble applic__nt with good charact__r refer__nces and relev__nt experi__nce

famil__r with differ__nt calculat__rs and comput__rs

techni____y compet__nt

trave___ing expen__es paid

excell__nt libr__y facilit__s avail__ble

© Michael Temple: Homework English   33   Spelling 3.5

EXPLANATION

What is a sentence?

- A sentence **makes sense** standing on its own.
- It starts with a **capital letter** and ends with **a full stop**, question mark or exclamation mark.
- It usually includes a **verb** with a **subject**.

A sentence never ends with a comma.

1 Making sense

Are you not sure where a sentence ends?
How can you tell if your 'sentence' is finished?

- Read it out.
- Ask yourself if it makes sense.
- Do the same thing with the next 'sentence'. (It might actually be part of the previous one.)

2 Simple sentences

A simple sentence contains a **subject** used with its **verb**. The subject is the person or thing doing the action (or being/feeling something):

Subject	verb	Subject	verb	
The rabbit	runs.	She	was	angry.

Sentences can contain several verbs:
The rabbit *scented* danger, *ran* and *leapt* down its burrow.
When she *was* angry her face *went* red.

3 A complete idea

It's a sentence if the idea is complete.

Parts of sentences	*Complete sentences*
… standing on its own	A sentence makes sense standing on its own.
When you have finished your sentence …	When you have finished your sentence you should put a full stop.

4 Short sentences

Sometimes, especially in commands and replies, sentences can be very short:
Stop! Help! ('You' is understood.)
No, thanks. (A previous comment is understood.)

5 Conversation

"I'm freezing," she said.
She said, "I'm freezing."
In these sentences the spoken words belong to the same sentence as 'she said'. (Note the commas.)

Sentence-building 4.1

© Michael Temple: Homework English

EXERCISES

What is a sentence?

1 Put extra large full stops and capital letters to show the beginning and end of these sentences.

(a) I checked the Geiger counter it was at danger level
(b) I woke at about six the sun was just rising
(c) Look up there it's John he's sitting on the garage roof
(d) I don't know what you're doing you shouldn't be here at this time it's the Christmas holiday, you know
(e) The twigs were damp he pulled his knife out his hands were numb he was frightened he banged his arms against his chest and leg it was bitterly cold the dog lay in the snow

2 Which of these commas should be full stops? Correct those that are wrong.

(a) She looked at her watch, it was five o'clock.
(b) Drugs could harm you, you could end up in hospital.
(c) Climbing the mountain, he lost all idea of time.
(d) All boats using the estuary must pay harbour dues, boat parking on the beach is available.
(e) Unless you promise to repay the money you borrowed last week, I shall have to tell your father.
(f) Whales used to be shot with harpoons, this meant they would die slowly.

3 How many sentences are there in each of these? Put full stops and capital letters where needed.

(a) No one knew what happened to him people say that he died
(b) He decided to warm up the biscuits and the bacon once they were nice and hot he started to eat the food
(c) He rose the sun streamed through the window lighting up the immense room with a golden glow which showed up every particle of dust
(d) The long day at last came to a close one by one the stars crept out in the inky sky the old man slumbered on beneath the hedge where he had lain all day he dreamt wonderful dreams of the past
(e) Buses will run on the number 9 route four times each hour except on Sundays

4 Correct these, writing each one out in the space.

(a) "I am leaving now," He said.

....

(b) The place was full of rubbish. Such as broken glass, litter and old tyres.

....

© Michael Temple: Homework English   35   Sentence-building 4.1

EXPLANATION

Phrases

Sentences are usually made up of phrases and clauses.

What is a phrase?
- A phrase is a group of words – at least two.
- It does not contain a verb with a subject.
- Unlike a sentence it does not have to make sense on its own.

1 Common forms of phrases

Here are some common ways in which we form phrases:
- Starting with a **preposition** such as 'in', 'on', 'under', 'with', 'by': *in* a phrase; *by* heart.
- Starting with an **infinitive** such as 'to see', 'to hear', 'to take': *to coin* a phrase; *to win* the cup.
- Using a **present participle** ending in '-ing' or **past participle** ending in '-ed': *choosing* his words carefully; *exhausted* by their efforts.
- Starting with an **adverb**: *immediately* after this.

2 What do phrases do?

- Phrases can do the work of **nouns**. They can be the subject or object of the verb.

  An old friend of mine came to see me yesterday.
  Learning pottery is fun.
  She hoped *to win the lottery*.

- Phrases can do the work of **adjectives**. They can tell you more about a noun or a pronoun.

  Charlie Chaplin, *the famous film comedian*, had a funny walk.
  With her heart beating loudly, she stood up to sing.

- Phrases can do the work of **adverbs**. They tell you more about the action, telling you when, where, how, why something happened.

She sat [under a tree] to read her book.

[At six o'clock,] we started our journey to the airport.

Sentence-building 4.2 © Michael Temple: Homework English

EXERCISES

Phrases

1 There are seven phrases in this passage. Underline them all,
Seville, a city in southern Spain, is famous throughout the world for its oranges and for its Spring carnival. In April people come out onto the streets to enjoy the Easter festivities.

2 Turn the words in italics into phrases,
e.g. She spoke *angrily*. She spoke *in an angry voice*.

(a) He's coming *soon*.

....

(b) The cows chewed the cud *repeatedly*.

....

(c) The snake climbed the wall *cautiously*.

....

3 Add a phrase to each of these sentences,
e.g. 'The girl went shopping.' You could add 'to buy a swimsuit'.

(a) He took a wrong turning   ....

(b) 'Star Trek' is a popular TV show   ....

(c) She spent all her money   ....

4 Join each pair of sentences by using a present participle, ending in '-ing', e.g.
I looked out of the window. I saw a woodpecker.
Looking out of the window, I saw a woodpecker.

(a) The boy sat on top of the haystack. He could see for miles.

....

(b) He thought there was no one about. He stole into the building.

....

(c) She put the jigsaw together. She was delighted with the result.

....

© Michael Temple: Homework English   Sentence-building 4.2

EXPLANATION

Problems with phrases

- Don't leave phrases hanging around.
- Make sure the phrase is attached to the right word.
- Don't put phrases in the wrong places.

1 Hanging phrases
Read this:

Animals are often badly treated. Thrown about. Kicked. Crushed in an overcrowded lorry for six hours or more. Arriving at the abattoir bruised and battered.

This reads like a set of notes and, apart from the first sentence, is a set of phrases left hanging in the air.

Now let's turn the phrases into a sentence:

They are thrown about, kicked, crushed in an overcrowded lorry for six hours or more, and finally arrive at the abattoir bruised and battered.

You should be able to spot hanging phrases if you read the passage aloud.

2 Wrongly attached phrases
Read this:

Climbing the mountain, we saw an eagle.

The phrase in italics before the comma correctly describes the subject: 'we' did the climbing.

But read this:

Looking out of the window, a hedgehog crossed the lawn.

This means the hedgehog was looking out of the window. The 'looking' needs to be related to its proper subject so the sentence should be: *Looking out of the window*, we saw a hedgehog crossing the lawn.

And what is wrong with this?
Coming downstairs, the door opened.

3 Wrongly positioned phrases
Be careful where you put a phrase.

Read this:

Macbeth kills Duncan while asleep *with a knife*.

The knife needs to go with Macbeth and the killing, not with Duncan and his sleep.
Better versions would be:
Macbeth kills Duncan *with a knife* while the king is asleep.
Or:
Macbeth kills the sleeping Duncan *with a knife*.

Sentence-building 4.3

EXERCISES

Problems with phrases

1 Insert these phrases in the right spaces.

to his dismay   Finding no one at home   on the door
at the lonely cottage   late in the evening

The traveller arrived .... in the forest .... and knocked

.... he knocked again even louder but .... there

was no reply.

2 Make these hanging phrases into proper sentences.

(a) Rushing about frantically. Not sure what he was doing. The man let the milk boil over.

(b) The electric trams started on their journey. Starting from the centre of the city. Going past the new shopping centre. Snaking up the hill. Through the university area. Overtaking most of the car traffic.

3 Using phrases containing participles, make each pair of sentences into one, e.g.

He saw an alligator. The alligator was crossing the road. He saw an alligator *crossing the road*. You need to decide whether to put the phrase first or not.

(a) He turned the corner. He bumped into the lamppost.

....

(b) She looked round. She saw a bull charging at her.

....

(c) He was left on his own. He didn't know what to do.

....

(d) She saw her favourite pop group on the TV. She turned up the volume.

....

(e) The game was played at great speed. The game was very exciting.

....

4 Correct these sentences.

(a) Gleaming in the night sky, the astronomer stared at the Pole Star.

....

(b) A UFO was detected by searchlights flying over Disneyland.

....

(c) Sitting on the bus, the Christmas lights looked inviting.

....

© Michael Temple: Homework English

Sentence-building 4.3

EXPLANATION

Clauses

- A clause is a group of words that contains a **verb** with its **subject**.
- There are two types of clause: **main** and **dependent**.

1 Subjects and verbs

The subject is the person or thing doing the action or being something:

… when she (subject) sings (verb) …

… although the player (subject) is (verb) injured …

2 Main clause

This is the key part or backbone of the sentence. It often makes a sentence on its own.

The man walked down the road …

I have a red and grey parrot …

3 Dependent clause

A dependent (also called subordinate) clause depends on the main clause. It doesn't make a sentence on its own. A dependent clause does the job of an adjective, adverb or noun.

- Doing the work of **adjectives**. Adjectives describe nouns.

    I have a *pretty* red and grey parrot.
    I have a red and grey parrot *which looks great*.
    adjective
    clause doing the work of an adjective

    Adjectival clauses usually begin with words like 'who', 'which', 'that' and 'whose'.

- Doing the work of **adverbs**. Adverbs tell us how, when, why, something happens.

    My parrot parks *neatly*.
    My parrot parks *so that it looks neat*.
    My parrot parks *as neatly as it can*.
    adverb
    clause doing the work of an adverb

    Adverbial clauses often begin with words like 'because', 'although', 'if', 'until', 'before'.

- Doing the work of **nouns**

    Parrots park on *perches*.
    This is *what parrots perch on*.
    noun
    clause doing the work of a noun

    Noun clauses usually begin with words like 'what' and 'whether', 'if', 'that', 'how' etc.

Sentence-building 4.4

© Michael Temple: Homework English

EXERCISES

Clauses

1 Join these pairs of sentences by using a clause starting with 'who', 'which', 'that'. You will need to decide which is the main idea, e.g.

The man was wearing a false beard. He was a spy.
The man *who was wearing a false beard* was a spy. Or:
The man *who was a spy* was wearing a false beard.

(a) The tennis players did really well in 1995. In 1996 they couldn't win a match.

....

(b) She liked the blue dress. The blue dress was on display in the window.

....

2 Turn the phrases in italics into clauses e.g.

The boy *in the red vest* won the race.
The boy *who was wearing the red vest* won the race.

(a) She managed to pass her exams *with the minimum of effort*.

....

....

(b) *Thinking there was no one in the house*, the burglar entered the bedroom window to search for jewellery.

....

....

3 Add a main clause to the beginning or end of these clauses, e.g.

When she awoke in the night + she saw a ghost.

(a) although the National Lottery has been hugely popular

....

....

(b) because people don't read much nowadays

....

....

4 Combine each pair of sentences into one, using an adverbial clause. e.g.

The door has only recently been painted. Please avoid touching it.
Please avoid touching the door *as (because) it has only recently been painted.*

(a) I was given the good news yesterday. I was in school at the time.

....

(b) She read a great deal. She enjoyed reading.

....

(c) The team scored on several occasions. However, they lost the game.

....

© Michael Temple: Homework English

Sentence-building 4.4

EXPLANATION

Using clauses

A clause contains a verb used with its subject.

dependent clause — When you read a long sentence *main clause* — you look out for the main clause *dependent clause* — that other clauses depend on.

1 Connecting words

There needs to be a link between your clauses. Starting your clauses with words such as 'who', 'although', 'because', 'if', 'when' and 'as' will show the connection between the clauses. It will also vary the pattern and flow of your sentences.

Here are some of the most common connecting words:

The shoes *that* I liked were expensive.
He worked *because* he wanted the job.
He worked *so that* he could get the job.
He worked *so* hard *that* he got the job.
They lost *though* they tried hard.
You'll win *if* you try hard.
I arrived *after* they'd gone.
They went *where* no one had gone before.
We played *as* well *as* I expected.
I can see *what* you are writing.

2 Go with the flow

Using clauses helps your writing to flow. Read this:

He went to the bank. He wanted to buy a trailer. He'd seen it in a local garage.

This would flow better if it read like this:

3 Changing the order

- When joining clauses you need to decide which is the main idea.
- To ring the changes, see how it would work to put the dependent clause at the beginning, in the middle or at the end of your main clause.

If you want to, you can often put a clause in different positions in a sentence.
You can often put a clause, if you want to, in different positions in a sentence.
You can often put a clause in different positions in a sentence, if you want to.

Sentence-building 4.5

EXERCISES

Using clauses

1 **You want to say that you will come to the party. You will need a lift. You don't have your own transport.**

Put these ideas into one sentence, using two of these words: 'if', 'because', 'though', 'unless'.

....

....

2 **Underline the connecting word which begins the dependent clause in each of these.**

(a) I gave my ticket to the attendant who showed me to my seat.

(b) She enjoyed French because she was good at it.

(c) When all else fails, try relaxation exercises.

3 **Join this up, using 'which', 'when' and 'if' in the right spaces.**

Groucho Marx was warned he'd be caught .... he didn't hide. He was told, "Duck

behind the sofa," .... he did. .... he reappeared he said, "There

was no duck behind the sofa."

4 **Move the dependent clause in each of these sentences into a different place. Write your sentence in the space beneath.**

(a) Other people came to the party whom I hadn't met earlier.

....

(b) So that you can stay fit, you should take regular exercise.

....

5 **Join the pairs of sentences choosing one of these words: 'although', 'because', 'as', 'while', 'when'**

(a) They were late. The film hadn't started.

....

(b) She became ill. She had eaten some mouldy vegetables.

....

(c) A parcel arrived yesterday. I was out at the time.

....

6 **Add a dependent clause before or after each of these main clauses.**

(a) You should work hard.

....

(b) Nothing can be done about it.

....

(c) The crowd cheered.

....

© Michael Temple: Homework English   43   Sentence-building 4.5

EXPLANATION
Paragraphs

When you put several sentences together you need to think about paragraphs. A paragraph is a connected passage of writing on one topic.

1 Showing where a paragraph begins
To show the beginning of a paragraph either start the first line a little way in from the margin (indenting), or leave a space between it and the paragraph before.

2 Planning paragraphs
You need to plan your work so that each paragraph is about a main idea. Arranging your notes under headings is a helpful way to plan your paragraphs. You also need to be sure that your paragraphs are arranged in a logical order.

Building a paragraph:
Start with a key or topic sentence. Add a series of sentences that expand upon or develop and illustrate the single main idea of the paragraph. End with a sentence that draws it all together.

Begin a new paragraph when you move on to the next main idea, etc.

3 Linking paragraphs
You can link your paragraphs with words such as 'secondly', 'therefore', 'however', or phrases like 'in addition', 'even more …'

Read this example of three connected paragraphs:

key sentence

(Volcanoes are clefts or splits in the earth's crust where molten lava or hot rock has erupted.) Their shape varies according to the nature of the rock. Some, like Mount Fuji in Japan, are composed of thick silica lava that results in a cone-shaped mountain with steep sides. Others, made from thinner, less sticky rocks like basalt, form mountains with gentler slopes, as in Iceland.

   Most of the world's volcanoes occur where plates of the earth's crust meet. The clash of these plates creates both volcanoes and earthquakes as, for instance, along the Pacific rim of North and South America where there is a string of volcanoes known as the 'ring of fire'.

   (However,) not all volcanoes are confined to the borders of crystal plates, since 'hot spots' have formed in other areas such as the Hawaiian Islands.

linking words

Sentence-building 4.6

© Michael Temple: Homework English

EXERCISES

Paragraphs

Write answers on a separate sheet.

1 **Rewrite this as one paragraph so that it reads fluently. Don't use 'and' more than once. You can join sentences, use phrases and clauses of different kinds, insert link words, rearrange ideas and vary the way you construct the sentence.**
The park was on three levels. One of them was a rain forest. This had huge waterfalls and trees in it. On the trees perched chipmunks. In big glass tanks there were black and white monkeys. Outside was a rose garden. It had ponds in the middle. One pond was full of carp. The others had swans, ducks and geese on them.

2 **Here are some random facts about cats. Sort them and then use the notes to write two paragraphs of varied, fluent sentences. Include all the facts given. You can, of course, change the wording and add link words.**
CATS: able to hear well ... different breeds...sharp canine teeth ... Persian, Siamese and Abyssinian all derive from African wildcat ... have sheathed claws ... learn hunting techniques through play ... can see well in the dark ... carnivorous animals ... belongs to the same family as the lion and the tiger ... have a keen sense of smell ... range in size from tiger to tiny African black-footed cat ... hunt at night ... agile

3 **First sort the following instructions into the correct order and then write one paragraph that contains all the points. Make sure it reads clearly and fluently.**
How to make an omelette:
(a) Add a little salt and pepper to the whisked eggs.
(b) Tilt the sides of the pan to spread the fat.
(c) Garnish the omelette with herbs and serve it immediately.
(d) Shift the pan backwards and forwards when eggs are in the pan.
(e) Melt a pat of butter or a little olive oil over a brisk heat in the pan.
(f) Crack three eggs and put the whites and yolks into a bowl.
(g) When the oil is hot pour the eggs carefully into the pan.
(h) Use either an omelette pan or a small frying pan.
(i) After allowing the mixture to set a little, tilt the pan away from you and fold the omelette into three.
(j) With a spatula draw the egg mixture in from the sides of the pan as it cooks.
(k) Turn the omelette into a pre-heated dish.
(l) Whisk the eggs thoroughly in the bowl.
(m) When the mixture in the pan is thick and creamy, spread it evenly over the surface of the pan.

© Michael Temple: Homework English

Sentence-building 4.6

EXPLANATION

Singular and plural agreement

Singular = one: I, he, she, a boy, a girl
Plural = more than one: we, they, the boys, the girls

1 Matching verb and subject

Some verb forms change for **singular** and **plural subjects**.

Singular (just one)		**Plural** (more than one)	
Subject	*verb*	*Subject*	*verb*
He	points	They	point
	is pointing		are pointing
	has pointed/was pointing		have pointed/were pointing
The ship	sinks/is sinking	The ships	sink
	has sunk/was sinking		are sinking
			have sunk/were sinking

2 Phrase as subject

It isn't always easy to see whether a phrase subject is plural or singular: '*A range* of goods *was* available' – the word 'range' is the real subject so the verb 'was' is singular.

3 Two subjects

- When two singular subjects are joined by 'and', the verb will be plural: *John and* I *are* brothers.
- If the two subjects are linked by 'with', 'as well as', 'accompanied by', the subject is singular and the verb is singular too: *The man*, accompanied by his wife, *was* walking along the road.

4 Either ... or and neither ... nor

Two singular subjects linked by these words are followed by a singular verb.
Either John *or* Susie *is* coming round today.
Neither the man *nor* his wife *was* talking.

If one or both subjects are plural, the verb is too:
Neither Steve *nor* his sisters *are* coming to the disco.

5 Singular or plural?

- **Collective nouns** (meaning groups of people or things):
  Usually you are thinking of the group as a whole, so use a singular verb: The crowd *was* huge.
  You might be thinking of individuals in a group, so then you use a plural verb: The police *were* quick on the scene.
- Some nouns are 'uncountable' and take a singular verb: There *was* milk everywhere. The food *has* gone bad.
- Some nouns look plural but are singular: Mathematics *is* my favourite subject. The news *was* very exciting.
- The words 'this', 'that', 'these' and 'those' agree with the noun they are attached to:
  this kind of music   *these* kinds of music
  that sort   *those* sorts

Common errors 5.1

46

© Michael Temple: Homework English

EXERCISES

Singular and plural agreement

1 Singular or plural? Choose the right word for the space.

(a) It is claimed that the number of immigrants (is/are) .... increasing.

(b) A full programme of social reforms (is/are) .... planned.

(c) The police (is/are) .... due for a pay rise.

(d) The Chairman of the Board, as well as the whole committee, (was/were) .... ready to resign.

(e) Almost one in ten students (leave/leaves) .... school without any exam passes.

(f) All along the coast (lie/lies) .... traces of the oil slick.

(g) A series of four amazing serves (was/were) .... enough to win the tennis match.

2 Correct the words in italics where necessary. Two are correct.

"Let's play a game," says S.

"Draughts *are* (..............................) boring," says D.

"Darts *is* (..............................) worse," says C.

"OK then, cards," says H.

Each of the players *are* (..............................) then dealt a hand of cards and they start playing. A sequence of four aces *are* (..............................) produced by S. This arouses D's suspicions.

"Let's see *them* (..............................) aces of yours," says D. "*There's* (..............................) two more in my hand, so this pack of cards *contain* (..............................) at least six of them."

"Someone *are* (..............................) cheating then," says S.

"One of my cards *is* (..............................) an ace, too," says H.

"Obviously it's one of *them* (..............................) joke packs," says S.

3 Aaargh! Correct this passage.

From the depths of the darkest dungeons emerge an eerie army of green-eyed ghouls. Every one of these grisly horrors have a ghastly glint in its gloating eye. The scaly skin and slimy skull of the foulest fiend glows in the shadows and then at its signal every one of these menacing monsters move towards us. And which of us know whether these kind of creatures are merely figments of our fearful minds?

EXPLANATION

Mind your verbs

1 'To have' not 'to of'
There is no verb 'to of'; even though it might sound like that when you speak.
Do not write: "I must of made a mistake."
You should write: "I must *have* made a mistake." (This can be shortened to 'must've' if you like.)

2 Watch your past and present
Check that you have the right mixture of tenses in any sentence:
Jem and Scout *were* Atticus's children. They *lived* (not 'live') in Maycomb. (Both verbs in past tense)
Robert *thinks* the bridge *is* (not 'was') not safe. (Both verbs in present tense)

3 To lie and to lay
To lie means to rest (intransitive) and **to lay** means to put an object down flat (transitive). (See 1.3 for transitive verbs.)

To lie	*To lay*
I lie down in the hammock	I lay the eggs on the table.
am lying	am laying
was lying	was laying
lay (past tense)	laid
have lain/have been lying	have laid/have been laying

4 Sitting and sat; standing and stood
'Was stood' or 'was sat' are colloquial forms, but in standard English you should write 'was standing' or 'was sitting'.

I am/was standing/I stood (not 'was stood') under a tree.
Standing (not 'stood') under a tree, I sheltered from the rain.

I am/was sitting/I sat (not 'was sat') under a tree.
Sitting (not 'sat') under a tree, I was attacked by ants.

5 Which past tense?
These past tenses and past participles sometimes cause problems:
to swim: I swam; I have swum
to run: I ran; I have run
to write: I wrote; I have written
to take: It took ages; It has taken
to sink: It sank; It has sunk
to flow: The water flowed, has flowed

to drink: I drank; I have drunk
to lend: He lent/was lent money
lean: she leant or leaned over, has leant
to fly: The bird flew, has flown
to sow: He sowed/has sown seeds.
to sew: She sewed/has sewn a button on.

Common errors 5.2

EXERCISES

Mind your verbs

1   Which of the verbs in italics is correct? Correct the others.

(a)   I have *took* (...............................) down that scruffy poster.

(b)   You must *of* (...............................) noticed the mess on the carpet.

(c)   All of us were *sat* (...............................) round the table.

(d)   The river has *overflown* (...............................).

(e)   The fox must *have* (...............................) put the hunters off the scent.

2   Correct these.

(a)   He realised that he has made a mistake.

....

(b)   She felt so ill that she has to lay down.

....

(c)   Rick boasted that he has five telephones in his house.

....

(d)   John said he is going to the cinema.

....

(e)   You should of checked what you have wrote.

....

3   Choose the correct word.

(a)   I (leant/lent) .... out of the window.

(b)   She (choose/chose) .... the red blouse.

(c)   They had obviously (drank/drunk) .... all the juice.

(d)   He (laid/lay) .... there for hours.

(e)   Two whales were (laying/lying) .... stranded on the beach.

(f)   I have just (sewed/sewn/sowed/sown) .... some lettuce.

(g)   It's not clear what he has (written/wrote) .... on the map.

(h)   The bell has just (rang/rung) .... for assembly.

(i)   Yesterday the guide (lead/led) .... them into the caves.

(j)   Since then much water has (flowed/flown) .... under the bridge.

4   Correct the errors in this story on a separate sheet of paper.

Stood on the deck, the boy saw his shipmates laying about being sick. They have obviously laid there for hours. The boy looks at the captain who had lent over the side to be sick. The boy panics, jumps into the ocean and swum to shore.

© Michael Temple: Homework English

49

Common errors 5.2

EXPLANATION

Comparatives and double negatives

1 Comparing two things or people (called the comparative)
We either add '-er' to the end of the adjective or put 'more' before it:

tall – tall*er*   clever – clever*er*   quick – quick*er*

beautiful – *more* beautiful   intelligent – *more* intelligent

TAKE CARE! Don't use both at once!

2 Comparing three or more things or people (called the superlative)
We either add '-est' to the end of the adjective or put 'most' before it:

the tall*est*   the clever*est*   the quick*est* of all three

the *most* beautiful   the *most* intelligent of them all

3 Some odd comparatives

good	better	best
bad	worse	worst
much	more	most
little	less	least

TAKE CARE! There is no such word as worser.

4 Points about comparisons
- When using 'as ... as' don't miss out the second 'as': This is as good *as* if not better than that.
- Don't mix up 'as' and 'than': older than me but as old as the hills.
- It may help to say what you are comparing with what. Don't just say cheaper milk, the best car, better service – better than what?
  This shop is offering *cheaper* milk *than* any other shop in town.
- 'Unique' means it's the only one like it. Strictly, things can't be more unique.

5 Few and less

Use 'few' when you can count the number.	Use 'less' when you can't count the amount.
a number of items	an amount of rice or sugar
a few eggs, few people	less rice, less sugar
fewer eggs, fewer people	the least chance
fewest of three or more items	

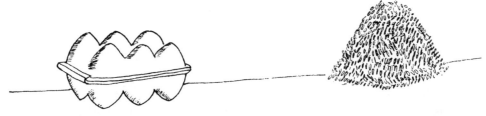

6 Double negatives
Double negatives may be used in idiomatic speech, but they are not usually acceptable in written standard English.
- So avoid writing 'I never eat no baked beans.'
- For the same reason don't use 'not' with 'hardly': I can (not 'can't') hardly walk.

Common errors 5.3   © Michael Temple: Homework English

EXERCISES

Comparatives and double negatives

1 Put the correct word in the space.

(a) Is London or Paris (further/furthest) .... from the sea?

(b) Which was the (more/most) .... interesting of the two countries you visited?

(c) Is the motorbike really more than twice as powerful (as/than) .... the new moped?

(d) Is she the (more elder/elder/eldest) .... of the three sisters?

(e) Is this the (less/least) .... costly of the two?

(f) Is this checkout for (less/fewer) .... than 8 items?

(g) Which of the two books do you think is (better/best) ....?

2 Avoid these double negatives by rewriting in the spaces.

(a) Nobody didn't do anything, miss.

....

(b) He couldn't hardly decide if the boys or the girls were the best behaved.

....

(c) She didn't know none of the answers.

....

(d) You don't know nothing yet.

....

(e) The second question was more trickier than the first.

....

(f) Nothing is worser than being unprepared.

....

3 The greatest yet! Correct these.

(a) Easily the best of the two 'Superman' films.

....

(b) More laughs but less thrills.

....

(c) 'Batman 2' is as exciting if not more exciting as 'Batman 1'.

....

....

....

(d) The most unique film I've ever seen. I've never seen nothing like it.

....

....

....

© Michael Temple: Homework English

Common errors 5.3

EXPLANATION
All in a twist

1 Some common mistakes

WRONG

✗ The reason/cause is *because* ...

✗ the sports for which we are famous *for*

✗ the law *to* which you referred *to*

✗ She was *equally clever as* her brother.

✗ His sound system *comprises of* several units.

RIGHT

The reason/cause is *that* ... ✓

the sports we are famous *for*
   or the sports *for which* we are famous ✓

the law *to which* you referred
   or the law which you referred *to* ✓

She was *as clever as* her brother.
   or She and her brother were *equally clever*. ✓

His sound system *consists of* several units.
   or His sound system *comprises* several units. ✓

2 A question of balance

WRONG

✗ neither he *or* she ...

✗ between this *or* that

✗ I *either suggest* you walk or catch the bus.

✗ She *both had* to earn a living and look after
   the house.

RIGHT

neither he *nor* she ✓

between this *and* that ✓

I suggest you *either walk* or catch the bus. ✓

She *had both* to earn a living and look after
   the house. ✓

3 And what should follow?

WRONG

✗ He had hardly started *than* the bell went.

✗ prefer this *than* that

✗ different *than*

✗ bored *of*

RIGHT

He had hardly started *when/before* the bell went. ✓

prefer this *to* that ✓

different *from* ✓

bored *with* ✓

4 The right place for it

● Be careful where you put the word 'only' or 'just'. The position can change the meaning.

He saw his grandfather *only* last week. (i.e. just recently)
He saw *only* his grandfather last week. (i.e. and no one else)
He *only* saw his grandfather last week. (This could mean several different things.)

● the three first chapters (Each book has only one first chapter.)
the first three chapters (This means chapters 1,2 & 3.)

Common errors 5.4

© Michael Temple: Homework English

EXERCISES
All in a twist

1 Sports shorts: Correct these sentences.

(a) Jamie only injured his leg last week but is fit already.
....

(b) This was a defeat from which the team will not recover from.
....

(c) The three first runners passed the post at ten-second intervals.
....

(d) Downie both won the high jump and the long jump.
....

(e) The players were hardly on court than the rain came down.
....

(f) She had to choose between the 100 metres or the 200 metres.
....

(g) His pole-vault technique was very different than anyone else's.
....

2 A rushed job: Correct this letter on a separate sheet (errors are in italics).

Hi. Late again. One reason is *because* I've been rushing around getting Kevin some new shoes. He took ages choosing and I got bored *of* the whole business. And in the end he said he preferred the old ones *than* the new.

Remember Mum's cough *of* which I told you *of* last time? Well, Dad finally got fed up *of* it and sent her to the doctor who told her she had a choice between smoking *or* bronchitis.
See you, Liz.

3 A bad report: Correct this passage on a separate sheet.

The school's central heating system which comprises of a boiler and fifty radiators is grossly inefficient. The chief cause of this is because the boiler is antiquated, though the radiators are almost equally as ineffective, being different than the standard type. Neither the boiler or the rest of the system has been properly maintained and I therefore either recommend installing a new system or at least a new boiler.

© Michael Temple: Homework English

Common errors 5.4

EXPLANATION

Twenty accident blackspots

Which of these do you get wrong?

1 *it's* = it is (or it has): *It's* mine. *It's* gone.
   its = of it, belonging to it: a dog without *its* tail

2 *there* = in that place: over *there*
   there is/are/were: *there was* a young lady from ...
   their = of them: taking *their* time. That's *their* funeral.
   they're = they are – *They're* off!

3 *there's* = there is (or there has): *There's* lots of it about.
   theirs = something belonging to them: That's *theirs*, not ours.

4 *where* (rhymes with air) = in what place: *Where* is it then?
   were (rhymes with fur) = past tense of are: We *were* lost.
   we're (rhymes with beer) = we are: *We're* short of cash.

5 *who's* = who is (or who has): *Who's* that? *Who's* done that?
   whose = belonging to whom: *Whose* car is that?

6 *your* = belonging to you: That is *your* problem.
   you're = you are: *you're* late again!

7 *to* = towards: *to* the zoo
   infinitive: *to* sing, *to* play, *to* do
   too = excessively: *too* hot, *too* much; also: You come, *too*.

8 *of* (say "ov") = belonging to: Queen *of* Hearts
   off (rhymes with cough) = from, down from: he fell *off* a cliff
   have = verb: I should *have* (or should've) known this. ('Of' isn't a verb.)

9 *lets*: He *lets* us talk.
   let's = let us: *Let's* go then.

10 *passed* = verb: He *passed* his exam; she has *passed* the corner.
    past: the *past*, *past* ages, went *past*, *past* caring

11 I lie/am lying/lay/have lain down for a rest.
    I lay/am laying/laid/have laid something down flat.

12 *lose* (rhymes with snooze) = can't find, don't win: win or *lose*.
    loose (rhymes with goose) = untied, not tight: a *loose* tooth

13 *affect* (can only be a verb) = to influence: Did it *affect* you?
    effect (noun) = a/the result: the *effect* was devastating.

14 *no* = not yes; *know* = be aware, have knowledge: I *know* how to ski.
    new = not old: no *new* ideas; *knew* = past tense of know: I *knew* her well.

15 *accept* (say Accept) = receive: I *accept* your offer.
    except (say Except) = without: all *except* one

16 *quiet* (say KWYET) = silent: Be *quiet*!
    quite (rhymes with right) = fairly, absolutely: *Quite* right!

17 *weather* = rain, sun, cloud, etc: What awful *weather*!
    whether = if: I don't know *whether* I can come.

18 *aloud* = out loud: Stop thinking *aloud*.
    allowed = permitted: No smoking *allowed*.

19 *principal* = chief: the *principal* points, the college principal
    principle = a law, rule, value: the *principle* of the thing

20 *practice* (noun): a games *practice*, doctor's *practice*
    practise (verb) to *practise*: You need to *practise* at tennis.

Common errors 5.5   © Michael Temple: Homework English

EXERCISES

Twenty accident blackspots

1 Cross out the words which are not correct.

(a) (Whose/Who's) that? (It's/Its) Jane. And (whose/who's) car is that? (It's/Its) hers and (it's/its) bumper is damaged. I don't know (whose/who's) done it but (it's/its) no business of mine.

(b) (Their/There/They're) not sure if (it's/its) (theirs/there's) or not, but (theirs/there's) no doubt (it's/its) not ours. (There/Their/They're) off to Australia but (where/we're/were) staying (where/we're/were) we always (where/we're/were).

(c) (It's/Its) in a class of (it's/its) own.

2 Choose the right word for the blank.

(a) I should (of/have/off/'ve) .... known better than to (of/have/off) ....
knocked the cup (of/have/off) .... the table.

(b) (Let's/Lets) .... see (weather/whether) .... we've (passed/past) .... our exams.

(c) No parking (allowed/aloud) .... Be (quiet/quite) .... (quiet/quite) .... in the library.

(d) If (your/you're) .... not (to/too) .... sure (whether/weather) .... to use 'loose' or 'lose', pronounce them.

(e) He had (laid/lain) .... the table while we had been (laying/lying) .... in the sun.

(f) I'll (accept/except) .... all offers (accept/except) .... that one.

(g) The car that just (passed/past) .... was (there's/theirs) ....

(h) They were (to/too) .... busy (to/too) .... attend to us.

(i) He must (of/have/off/'ve) .... gone (passed/past) .... us.

(j) (You're/Your) .... off for (you're/your) .... holidays, are you?

3 Choose the right word for the blank.

(a) More people have (passed/past) .... their exams in the (passed/past) .... few years.

(b) This tooth is so (loose/lose) .... that I'll (loose/lose) .... it.

(c) My (principle/principal) .... concern was over a matter of (principle/principal) ....

(d) The (effect/affect) .... of the tragedy was that she was (effected/affected) by blindness.

(e) The building (sight/site) .... was hardly a (sight/site) .... for sore eyes.

(f) (Practise/Practice) .... makes perfect.

(g) I don't know (weather/whether) .... the (weather/whether) will be good today.

(h) I (knew/new) .... you'd bought a (knew/new) coat but didn't (know/no) .... it was so expensive.

© Michael Temple: Homework English   55   Common errors 5.5

EXPLANATION
Using a dictionary and thesaurus

1 Using a dictionary
A good dictionary not only gives you the meaning or meanings of a word, it also gives additional information which can help improve both your reading and writing skills. For example:

phonetic alphabet to show how the word is pronounced

part of speech (*n* = noun; *vb* = verb)

definition of different meanings

host (həʊst) *n*. 1. a person who receives or entertains guests: All the party guests said he was the perfect host. 2. the compere of a show or television programme. 3. Biol. an animal or plant that supports a parasite. 4. *vb* to act as the host

example of use of the word

2 Using a thesaurus
A thesaurus is a reference book which lists words of similar meaning, also known as **synonyms**. A thesaurus is particularly useful for improving writing skills. It can help you to find the most appropriate word for the meaning you wish to convey.

If you look up the adjective 'proud' in a thesaurus, the following synonyms are likely to be among those listed:

arrogant; haughty; self-satisfied; grand; majestic; honoured.

The words are similar, but carry slightly different meanings for use in different contexts. For example, the first three words would be used to show **disapproval**: 'arrogant' means being conceited/having an over-high opinion of oneself; 'haughty' usually refers to someone having high and mighty manners; 'self-satisfied' means being smug/too pleased with oneself. The other three words suggest **approval**: 'grand' is impressive and dignified; 'majestic' is even grander, like a king or queen; 'honoured' means a feeling of pride or privilege, for example on receiving a prize.

3 The right word in the right place
A dictionary or thesaurus can help guide your choice of word when writing. You want to know, for instance, if the word:
- has the exact shade of meaning you want
- can be used in this context
- fits in with the style and purpose of the writing (for example, informal or formal)
- has the right tone.

Misuse of words can confuse your meaning. For example:
- choosing a word with the wrong associations for your purpose:
  e.g. The drains had an unpleasant *aroma*.
  Use the words 'smell or 'odour'. 'Aroma' is used to refer to a pleasant smell.

- using a word or phrase that doesn't fit the style and context:
  e.g. Customers are requested not to permit their *kids* to climb on the trolleys.
  Use 'children'. 'Kids' is too informal in this context: advice or request to supermarket customers.

- choosing a word that has the wrong sense or isn't used in this way:
  e.g. He hoped to *replenish* his lost youth.
  Use 'recapture' or 'regain'. 'Replenish' means 'to fill up again'.

Vocabulary skills 6.1

© Michael Temple: Homework English

EXERCISES

Using a dictionary and thesaurus

1 Find a synonym for each word in italics.

(a) The management and the union will not come to an agreement unless one side *modifies* its demands.

(b) Her *prowess* at volleyball makes it certain that she'll be chosen for the Olympic team.

(c) The *imposing* building in front of you is the headquarters of the World Bank.

(d) The most *eminent* surgeons carried out the operation on the prince's ingrown toenail.

(e) The lost dog had a *forlorn* expression on its face.

(f) The *submerged* rocks are dangerous to shipping when the tide goes out.

2 Choose the most appropriate verb from the list in the box for each of the situations below. (Note: some verbs may fit more than one situation.)

sidle	amble	totter	trudge
stagger	strut	march	lurch

(a) a baby just learning to walk

(b) a drunk walking down the street

(c) a weary farmer returning home through the mud

(d) two teenagers guiltily approaching someone

(e) someone who has just been shot

(f) a lazy walk in the country

(g) a model walking down the catwalk

(h) someone going to the manager of a hotel to make a strong complaint

3 Choose the most appropriate word for each space.

There seemed to be a loud .... (sound, bang, thud) and a blinding .... (beam, ray, flash) of light all .... (round, beside, behind) me and I felt a tremendous shock – no pain, only a violent .... (shock, agony, feeling), such as you get from an electric terminal; with it a sense of .... (perfect, utter, entire) weakness, a feeling of being stricken and .... (reduced, shrivelled, squeezed) up to nothing. The sand-bags in front of me .... (sank, dropped, receded) into .... (huge, gigantic, immense) distance. I fancy you would feel much the same if you were .... (zapped, attacked, struck) by lightning.   (George Orwell)

4 Look at the words in the box.

intoxicated	plenty of	extremely pleased	theft
over the moon	a considerable amount of	nicking	pissed
really chuffed	lots of	drunk	stealing
inebriated	delighted	purloining	oodles of

(a) Sort the words above into four groups according to their sense.

(b) Grade the words according to how formal or informal they are, as follows:

INFORMAL ....FORMAL

(Slang to chatty)   (neutral)   (Fairly formal to formal)

© Michael Temple: Homework English   Vocabulary skills 6.1

EXPLANATION

Express yourself better

Improving your vocabulary skills can help you to express yourself better in your writing. It helps to remember that effective use of words doesn't always mean using long words or clever expressions.

1 Replace overworked words
Words like 'get', 'got', 'nice', 'good' and 'great' are often overworked or loosely used so that they become vague and monotonous. Think of another word.

2 Avoid words and phrases which are too informal
Phrases like 'a lot of', 'a bit of', 'kind of' and 'sort of' are generally too 'chatty' for formal writing like essays and business letters. Be precise, for example, try using 'many' or 'much' instead of 'a lot of'.

3 Avoid clichés
Clichés are expressions or ideas that have become stale from overuse. For example:
'In this day and age' clichés are 'as dead as a doornail'. They 'fall flat as a pancake', usually 'on deaf ears'. It 'goes without saying' that they should be avoided 'like the plague'.

4 Avoid using words that repeat the main meaning
In these examples, the bracketed words are not needed:
(advance) planning; (end) result; (usual) custom; (mutual) co-operation; the (ever-increasing) number of unemployed is growing every day.

5 Don't use too many words
Using too many words can sound clumsy and make your meaning less clear to the reader. For example:
'owing to the fact that' – replace with 'because' or 'since'
'had occasion to be' – replace with 'was'
'in this day and age' or 'at the present moment in time' – replace with 'now' or 'today'

6 Don't try too hard to impress
Don't dress up what you want to say in pompous or long-winded language just to impress. For example:
'The audience signified their approbation of the vocal artist by an appreciative manual response.'
This means: The audience clapped the singer.

 Some words are commonly misused. For example, the word 'literally' means 'in actual fact'. You can't 'literally fly down the street on your bike' (unless you sprout wings!).

Vocabulary skills 6.2 © Michael Temple: Homework English

EXERCISES

Express yourself better

Write your answers on a separate sheet.

1 Rewrite the following without using the words 'get' and 'got' more than once. Use a different replacement word each time. You may prefer to change the whole sentence, as long as the meaning stays the same.

On the morning of my first day at school I got up early and got dressed while my mother got the breakfast. After that I got my pen and pencil and got my new cap from the hook. Having got himself a map, dad had already got to know the way to school. Once in the car, however, we soon found we had got into a traffic jam and it was obvious that we would be lucky to get to school on time.

When we eventually got there, I got a nasty shock – there was no one there. We had got the day wrong!

2 Choose a better adjective to replace 'good' in each of these phrases.

a good idea; good weather; of good character; a good shot; a good performance; a good meal; a good film.

3 Read this passage which is full of clichés.

In this day and age we must explore every avenue and leave no stone unturned in an all-out attempt to avoid another catalogue of disasters. Phrases like stand up and be counted and more than meets the eye are just the thin end of the wedge. If the worst comes to the worst we must go back to the drawing board and start again from scratch. It will be a mammoth task and it's easier said than done but even at the eleventh hour we can sow the seeds of clearer thinking and expression if we avoid all clichés like the plague.

(a) Underline all the clichés you can find. There are 16.

(b) Rewrite the last sentence without using any clichés.

4 Reduce each of these phrases to a single word.

at an early date; at this moment in time; ahead of schedule; am in possession of; was of the opinion that; in the event that; on the grounds that.

5 Rewrite these sentences so that they are clear and accurate.

(a) It was literally raining cats and dogs.

(b) Hang-gliding is quite a unique experience.

(c) The end result was a victory for the home team.

6 Rewrite this over-complicated sentence in clear, simple English, using between 15 and 20 words.

In the not unlikely event of your son's failure to comply with the school's expectations in regard to attendance at cricket practice sessions, action may be needed to be taken to exclude him from consideration when the time comes for team selection.

© Michael Temple: Homework English

Vocabulary skills 6.2

EXPLANATION
Using imagery

Language can be used **literally** to describe what actually happened, for example:
The bird flew down the avenue.
It can also be used **figuratively** when an idea is pictured and a comparison is suggested, for example:
The boy flew down the street on his new bike.
(He didn't actually fly, but moved fast and easily like a bird.)

1 Similes

A simile brings out a point (or points) of likeness or similarity between two different things. It begins with the word *like* or *as*:
His hand was trembling *like a leaf*.
Her skin was *as white as snow*.
The old man turned his head *like an old tortoise in the sunlight*.
A simile not only helps you picture and sense the idea, but can also express feelings or attitudes. How does Robert Burns feel about his girlfriend when he writes:
'O my love is like a red, red rose
That's newly sprung in June...'?

2 Metaphors

A metaphor makes comparisons by imagining one thing as if it were another. For example:
The train snaked its way up the mountain pass.
(The train is pictured as a snake twisting its way slowly up the mountain.)
Anger flared up in her face. (Anger is compared with or pictured as red fire.)

3 Personification

This is a kind of metaphor where an object or an idea is treated as if it were alive or a person. For example:
Father Time
Justice holds the scales.
Fortune smiled on us.

4 Imagery

Writers often use imagery (or 'picture-language') to create vivid pictures and sensations in the mind. Imagery may include similes, metaphors and personification. Here, Shakespeare's Macbeth, hearing of his wife's death, describes life like this:

    Out, out, brief candle!
Life's but a walking shadow, a poor player
That struts and frets his hour upon the stage
And then is heard no more. It is a tale
Told by an idiot, full of sound and fury,
Signifying nothing.
(Life is a candle, a shadow, a poor actor, an idiot's tale. It means nothing.)

- If you start with one metaphor or 'picture-idea', stay with it. Don't start mixing metaphors, as in this example:
The policeman ironed out the bottleneck.
- Some metaphors and similes are used so frequently that they become clichés. For example:
She shot out of the room, as quick as a flash.

Vocabulary skills 6.3

© Michael Temple: Homework English

EXERCISES

Using imagery

Write answers to questions 3 to 5 on a separate sheet.

1 Underline the metaphors in these sentences.

(a) The saw snarled as the men cut down the tree.

(b) Death lays his icy hand on kings.

(c) He may have been a lion among men but she had nerves of steel.

(d) That boy is a tiger in the tackle.

(e) He wormed his way into our confidence.

2 Underline all the metaphors and similes you can find in this passage describing a fire on a mountainside.

Smoke was rising here and there among the creepers that hung from the dead or dying trees. As the boys watched, a flash of fire appeared at the root of one wisp, And then the smoke thickened. Small flames stirred at the bole of a tree and crawled away through leaves and brushwood, dividing and increasing. One patch touched a tree trunk and scrambled up like a bright squirrel. The squirrel leapt on the wings of the wind and clung to another standing tree, eating downwards. Beneath the dark canopy of leaves and smoke the fire laid hold on the forest and began to gnaw. At the sight of the flames and the irresistible course of the fire, the boys broke into shrill, excited cheering. The flames crept as a jaguar creeps on its belly towards a line of birch-like saplings that fledged an outcrop of pink rock.

(adapted from *Lord of the Flies* by William Golding)

3 Write two sentences, each using a simile to describe someone's hair or face.

By your choice of simile make the description sound attractive in the first sentence and unattractive in the second.

4 Make up a fresh or unusual metaphor or simile to express a similar idea to those listed below.

For example, 'plain as a pikestaff' could become 'as inconspicuous as a tarantula on a slice of angel food'.

(a) She was as cool as a cucumber.

(b) The news spread like wildfire.

(c) He was a tower of strength.

(d) Life's just a bed of roses.

(e) She was as hard as nails.

5 Use imagery (including, if you like, metaphors, similes and personification) to write a vivid description of one of these.

Try to develop your 'picture-ideas' in about three sentences.

winter	freedom	misery	fog
wind	storm	anger	poverty
heat	the sea		

© Michael Temple: Homework English

Vocabulary skills 6.3

EXPLANATION

Polish your style

There are many different ways a writer can use language to produce different effects. For example, poets often use repeated vowel and consonant sounds; people making speeches may use particular patterns or repeat memorable words and phrases; newspaper reporters or advertising copywriters often use word-play, such as puns.

1 Using sounds for effect

- **Onomatopoeia**: here the writer uses words that imitate the sound of the thing described, for example:

  'the stuttering rifles' rapid rattle' (Wilfred Owen)

- **Alliteration**: here the writer repeats the same consonants:

  'The fair breeze blew, the white foam flew,
  The furrow followed free … '(Coleridge)
  'six scrumptious sausages sizzling in a pan'
  'murmuring of innumerable bees' (Tennyson)

- **Assonance**: here vowel sounds are repeated to echo the sound or sense:

  '...tired eyelids upon tired eyes' (Tennyson)
  (The repeated 'i' sounds create a sleepy effect.)

2 Ordering or balancing words for effect

- **Balance and contrast**, for example: 'To err is human; to forgive divine '(Pope)
  'We have just enough religion to make us hate, but not enough to make us love one another.' (Swift)

- **Climax or the 'ladder' effect**: this often involves repeating words or phrases, using contrast and building up to a powerful climax, as in Martin Luther King's famous speech 'I have a dream':

  '… I have a dream that one day even the state of Mississippi, a state sweltering with the heat of injustice, sweltering with the heat of oppression, will be transformed into an oasis of freedom and justice. I have a dream that my four little children will one day live in a nation where they will not be judged by the colour of their skin but by the content of their character. I have a dream today.'

- **Rhetorical questions**: these are questions that expect no answer, but are used for effect and to involve an audience: 'And is this what we are born to? Are we not free?'

3 Word-play

- **A pun** is a play on words, either on two meanings of the same word or on words sounding alike, for example: 'Drilling holes is boring.'
  Puns are often used in news headlines and advertisements.

- **A paradox** is a saying that seems to be nonsense and seems to contradict itself. It does, in fact, have a point:
  'More haste, less speed.'

- **Exaggeration or hyperbole** is a way of stressing something and can often be used humorously:
  He ate mountains of pasta.
  Supper took absolutely ages.

- **Understatement** can also be used for effect:
  The tough-guy hero described his fatal wound as a mere scratch.

- **A euphemism** is a mild or indirect way of referring to something unpleasant or embarrassing:
  She passed away last night.

- **An innuendo** is a sly or nasty hint:
  He 'accidentally' shredded all evidence of his guilt.

Vocabulary skills 6.4 · © Michael Temple: Homework English

EXERCISES

Polish your style

Write your answers on a separate sheet.

1 Use onomatopoeia, alliteration or assonance to describe any three of these. Write at least one sentence for each.

a sound you dislike   a sound you like   snakes
leaves in a breeze   the roar of the traffic   fire
footsteps in the snow   a police siren   seagulls
a jet aeroplane   windscreen wipers   heartbeats

2 Write, or collect, three newspaper headlines or advertisements that use alliteration and/or puns for effect.

3 Make up a title (for example, for a musical or for a shop) using either a pun or alliteration.

4 Make up or collect three puns in a similar question-and-answer format.

E.g. Q: What is a royal thunderstorm?
     A: One that reigns/rains over us.

5 Use balance and contrast to complete these sentences in your own words

(as in 'United we stand; divided we fall').

(a) To .... is better than to ....

(b) .... has few .... but .... has many ....

(c) Many ....; few ....

6 'Playing it cool' and 'Going over the top'

(a) Write one sentence using understatement to describe some great or famous achievement.

(b) Write one sentence using exaggeration to describe some unimportant or trivial action.

7 What do these euphemisms mean?

budget-price; the smallest room in the house; for the fuller figure; a refuse-disposal officer; public amenity facility

8 Explain the innuendo in these.

(a) Julian received promotion in just one month: his father was the chairman of the firm.

(b) The criminal wore a purple jacket. The garment looked remarkably like yours, Mr Smith.

9 Write a short speech, or the last section of a speech, in which you argue strongly for or against a controversial issue.

(for example, animal rights, the monarchy, the death penalty, euthanasia).
Write about half a page, using some of the devices described in the Explanation. Think about how you will give your speech a powerful ending.

© Michael Temple: Homework English   Vocabulary skills 6.4

Answers

1 *Parts of speech*

1.1 The naming of parts:

1 (a) quick, brown, lazy   (b) orange, tiny, timid   (c) all, equal

2 verbs: was, hung; nouns: girl, eyes, hair, shoulders; adverb: loosely; adjectives: tall, blue (also her) pronoun: she; prepositions: with, over

3 1 – pronoun, 2 – verb, 3 – adjective, 4 – noun, 5 – conjunction, 6 – preposition, 7 – indefinite article, 8 – noun, 9 – adjective, 10 – verb, 11 – adverb, 12 – adjective

4 (a) middle/south (noun)   (b) team (noun)   (c) beautiful/exciting etc. (adjective)

5 (a) adjective   (b) noun   (c) preposition   (d) verb

6 conjunctions: and, but, because, and

7 1 – adjective; 2 – noun; 3 – verb; 4 – verb; 5 – preposition; 6 – noun

1.2 Pronouns:

1 (a) I   (b) me   (c) we   (d) her   (e) he

2 (a) He and I   (b) Tom and she   (c) you and he   (d) Zeinab and me   (e) We poor   (f) and me

3 (a) Either: You must … your or: One must … one's   (b) The rose is … and (it) grows (or Roses are … plants and (they) grow)   (c) Cars have … for them (or The car has … for it)

(d) because he or she wants, or Readers read on.

4 (a) person whom (or that or who)   (b) She and I   (c) you have … you tend … to use it

(d) sister and me

1.3 Verb forms:

1 Either: It is … throw … owls are hooting … Badgers are starting … Hedgehogs are shuffling … family sleep Or: It was … trees threw … owls were hooting … Badgers started … Hedgehogs shuffled … family slept.

2 (a) English is taught.   (b) Grapes are grown …   (c) The house was broken into by burglars.

3 had(T) swam(I) climbed(T) walked(I) laughed(I) ate(T) sang(T) cried(I) left(I)

4 (a) to avoid the pedestrian   (b) to eat … to drink

5 e.g. (a) … the driver skidded into the ditch.   (b) … man went to see his doctor

(c) … the burglar climbed through the window   (d) driver crashed into the wall

(e) the boxer got up to win the fight.

1.4 Conjunctions:

1 Yesterday at the wild-life park (or: when I went to the wild-life park) I saw the monkeys, zebras and lions. After lunch (or: after I'd had lunch) and a bumpy ride on a camel, I looked at a few more animals before going home (or: before I went home).

2 Waking early, I got out of bed, washed and ate my breakfast before setting off for school and meeting some friends (or: before I set off for school and met some friends).

3 As it was raining, we decided to go to town for the day to take the rabbits to my grandma who gave us some money which we spent in town.

4 If a pregnant mother smokes, the child can be small, and if the father smokes, his sperm can be abnormal. Non-smokers, on the other hand, carry little risk of getting lung cancer.

5 Terrified he'd be caught, the burglar climbed hastily out of the window without noticing the water-butt beneath him. He became stuck in the water-butt and was caught by a passing policeman.

6 A girl went to a night club, proudly wearing her new £500 ring, but, as it was loose on her finger, it fell off without her noticing until the following day. Heart-broken, she reported the loss to the police, but on returning (or when she returned) later to the night club she noticed something glinting on the ground. It was her ring – quite undamaged.

© Michael Temple: Homework English

2 *Punctuation*

2.1 Capitals:

1 (a) Dave Did Wolverhampton Wanderers Manchester United F.A. Cup

(b) The English Channel French Calais English Dover Folkestone

(c) I've 'Animal Farm' English George Orwell American 'Of Mice and Men' John Steinbeck

(d) The teacher ... I don't ... 'Mother Nature'   (e) Dr Jones 'A. Jones M.D.'

(f) It wasn't ... Joe Potsky ... C.I.A. K.G.B.

2 (a) My Gemma. I Gemini I've 'Daily Wail' It Thursday Perhaps I'll National Lottery

(b) What's Australia Jim Sydney George I Melbourne Jo At Julie Well It's Canberra

(c) My ... My ... 'I Will Always Love You' Whitney Houston 'Redemption Song' Bob Marley I replied Yeah I prefer 'A Hard Day's Night' the Beatles

(d) Dear Parents, This Christmas 'West Side Story' Leonard Bernstein Puerto-Ricans New York. It Shakespeare Theatre Tuesday December Saturday December.

2.2 Ending the sentence:

1 (a) Sam woke. He ... temperature. It ... freezing. He ... nose. It ... more.

(b) To find ... to yourself. You ... ends. Each ... own.

(c) On ... house. It was brilliant. He ... auction. It ... condition.

(d) Nick's shaky. He ... slowly. He ... fish.

(e) When ... dismayed them. They ... touch it. Some ran away. (or ;) Some ... body. They ... them. Others ... womb. One ... moving.

2 (a) It ... raining. The rain ... trees. Water ... path.

(b) Kino ... shell. Through ... hard. He ... apart. The lip-like ... subsided. Kino ... moon.

3 Help! sinking. (or !) hear me? ... he's doing. you did it. seemed to know. so puzzled?

2.3 Commas:

1(a) chips, peas, kippers, pasta   (b) came, I saw,   (c) Giggs, the United striker,

(d) "Friends, Romans, countrymen, your ears,"   (e) Well, now, haven't you, Steve?   (f) here, Kevin?

(g) is, as anyone can see, full of humour, horror, ghosts,   (h) Lincoln, President ... States,

(i) no idea," she said, "what ...

2 (a) Dear Jo, Saturday, playing ... beach, swimming ... barbecue. The next day, however, was a disaster, just ... wrong. As ... morning (,) we ... country, getting ... lunch. Finally, and worst of all, ... Well, that's life, I suppose. Can't ... see you, Pam.

(b) Wilde, when ... morning, said, "I ... comma." When ... afternoon, he replied, "I ... out."

3 (a) ... at all – buckets –   (b) fruits (oranges ... limes)   (c) summer – it ... August –

4 (a) Did you call, Alex? (asking Alex if he called)

(b) Mrs Davis, the teacher is late. (telling Mrs D that the teacher is late)

2.4 Apostrophes:

1 (a) the monkey's paw   (b) the monkeys' paws   (c) the children's games   (d) a week's holiday

(e) the lorries' exhausts   (f) the people's votes   (g) the Chairman of the Water Board's speech

(h) the baker's shop   (i) the Prime Minister's wife   (j) for Jesus' sake

2 I don't we're can't Sue's won't Anne's It's isn't it? they're aren't they? I'd have (I would've) no one's there's Let's doesn't we've

3 (a) videos computers prices   (b) There's cooks   (c) Who's What's Where's

(d) It's hers yours Sam's brother's   (e) Didn't men's children's ladies' coats

(f) car's bumper's its driver's   (g) Don't you're

2.5 Inverted commas:

1 (a) "I'm ... parrot," says   (b) Pop star says, "I just ... alone."   (c) "I want ... ambassador," says

(d) correct

2 (a) Paragraph: Jane ... friends, "What's ... soap?" New paragraph: "I like 'Eastenders'," replied Kate, "because ... situations." New paragraph: "Maybe," said Gareth, "but ... 'Coronation Street' ... characters." New paragraph: Jane answered, "Yes, but I prefer 'Neighbours'. tune: 'Good ... friends'."

(b) Paragraph: "I don't ... doing, Alex," said Simon, "but it isn't the proper homework, is it?"

New paragraph: "I think ... semi-colon," replied Alex.

New paragraph: "You ... well," Simon pointed out.

Answers

2.6 Colons and semi-colons:

1 (a) ... ingredients: ... free-range; ... tomatoes;   (b) exam: one ... red; highlighter;

2 (a) begins: "To be ...   (b) ... factory: his father   (c) emphasise this: we all

3 mid-October; shining; suit; trouble; empty;

4 (a) itself; (or :) it   (b) tent; you   (c) country; (or :) they   (d) threatening: storm gathering; panes;

5 (a) laws – laws   (b) again – by   (c) Nevis – but

6 full-time computer-literate (the other two could also be hyphenated)

3 Spelling

3.1 Spelling strategies:

7 basically, friend, rein, committed, surprise; across, immediately, laid, paid, vicious, freight, argument, seize, separated, receive, beginning

3.2 Say as you spell:

1 receive, grief, neighbours, priest, leisure, niece, belief, deceive, relieve, conceited

2 (a) planning, barring, staring, starring, sloping, reciting

(b) wrapped, described, pined, skimmed, pinned, excited

3 (a) referring, orbiting, omitting, occurring, quarrelling, offering

(b) suffered, offered, expelled, targeted, cancelled, admitted

4 outrageous, noticeable, serviceable, mimicked

5 mischief, seize, preferred, receive, foreign, religious, reign, committed, occurred, excitement

3.3 It's not always how it sounds:

1 scenic, telephone, knowledge, physics

2 surprise, tombstone, government, chocolate, uninterested, quarter, February, Wednesday

6 (a) must license ... dog licence   (b) singing practice ... will practise

7 in front of; a lot of; cannot; although; in spite of; lots of; as well; tomorrow; whereas; everywhere; in fact; no one (or no-one); in between

3.4 Word-building:

2 disappoint, unnecessary, misunderstanding, unnatural, dissimilar, mislaid

3 arrange, announce, approve, abbreviate, correct, commemorate, commit, corrupt, illegible, immature, irrelevant, irresistible, opposition, occur, suppose, suffix

4 (a) management, excitement, advertisement, achievement

(b) meanness, keenness, happiness, liveliness

(c) careful, successful, pitiful, beautiful

(d) hopeless, clueless, careless, pitiless

5 carrying, carried, journeying, journeyed, marrying, married, pitying, pitied, envying, envied, replying, replied, satisfying, satisfied

3.5 Endings, or suffixes:

1 occasionally, beautifully, skilfully, improbably, humbly, tragically, immediately, luckily, actually, automatically, merrily, separately, successfully, horribly

2 roofs, halves, potatoes, glasses, videos, jockeys, lorries, valleys, factories, batteries, sandwiches, ponies

3 author, familiar, further, secondary, compulsory, cemetery, luxury, politician, possession, profession, religious, courageous, different, relevant, sentence, visible

4 faithfully, sincerely, peculiar, emperor, noticeable, scientifically, changeable, irresistible, responsible, visitor

5 (a) doctor's surgery; solicitor's secretary; laboratory technician; gardener; surveyor; professor; scholar; musician; voluntary; vehicle maintenance supervisor

(b) responsible applicant character references relevant experience familiar different calculators computers technically competent travelling expenses excellent library facilities available

© Michael Temple: Homework English   **Answers**

4 Sentence-building

4.1 What is a sentence?:

1 (a) … counter. It was … level.   (b) … six. The sun … rising.   (c) there. It's John. He's … roof.
(d) … you're doing. You … time. It's … know.
(e) … damp. He … out. His … numb. He was … frightened. He … leg. It … cold. The … snow.
2 (a) … watch. It …   (b) … harm you. You …   (c) correct   (d) … dues. Boat …   (e) correct
(f) harpoons. This
3 (a) No one … to him. People … died.   (b) He … bacon. Once … food.   (c) He rose. The sun … dust.
(d) The long … close. One … sky. The old … all day. He … past.   (e) Buses … Sundays.
4 (a) "I am leaving now," he said.   (b) The … rubbish, such as … tyres.

4.2 Phrases:

1 a city in Southern Spain … throughout the world … for its oranges … for its Spring carnival … In
April … onto the streets … to enjoy the Easter festivities
2 e.g. (a) in a moment   (b) again and again   (c) with caution
3 e.g. (a) Thinking about the meeting he took a wrong turning at the traffic lights
(b) "Star Trek", the long-running science fiction series, is …
(c) In a fit of extravagance she spent all her money on the first day.
4 (a) Sitting on top …, the boy could see …   (b) Thinking there was no one about, he stole …
(c) After putting the jigsaw together, she was delighted …

4.3 Problems with phrases:

1 at the lonely cottage … late in the evening … on the door. Finding no one at home … to his dismay
2 (a) Rushing … frantically, not … doing, the man … over.
(b) Starting on their journey from the city centre, the electric trams went past the new shopping
precinct, then, snaking up the hill, passed through the university area, overtaking most of the car
traffic.
3 (a) Turning the corner, he …   (b) Looking round, she …   (c) Left on his own, he didn't …
(d) Seeing her … TV, she   (e) Played at great speed, the game …
4 (a) The astronomer stared at the Pole Star gleaming …
(b) A UFO flying over Disneyland was detected by …
(c) Sitting on the bus, we thought the Christmas lights looked …

4.4 Clauses:

1 (a) The tennis players, who did really well in 1995, couldn't win … in 1996.
(b) She liked the blue dress which was …
2 (a) … though she made little effort   (b) After he had looked around, the burglar …
3 (a) … popular, people's contributions to charities have dropped.   (b) Fewer books are sold because …
4 (a) I was given the good news yesterday while I was …
(b) She read a great deal because she enjoyed reading.
(c) The team scored on several occasions, even though they lost …

4.5 Using clauses:

1 I'd like to come to the party, though I'll need a lift because I don't have my own transport.
2 (a) who   (b) because   (c) When
3 if which When
4 (a) Other people, whom I hadn't met earlier, came …
(b) You should take regular exercise so that you can stay fit.
5 (a) Although they were late the film hadn't started.
(b) She became ill because she had eaten some mouldy vegetables.
(c) A parcel arrived yesterday while I was out.
6 e.g. (a) … hard so that you pass your exams. (b) Although the situation seems most unfair, nothing …
(c) cheered when the President appeared.

Answers

4.6 Paragraphs:

1 The park was on three levels, one of which was a rain forest that contained huge waterfalls and trees with chipmunks perched in them. There were black and white monkeys in big glass tanks, while outside there was a rose garden with ponds in the middle. One pond was full of giant carp whereas the others had swans, ducks and geese on them.

2 Cats belong to the same family as lions and tigers and range in size from the tiny African black-footed cat to the tiger. Different breeds include the Persian, the Siamese and the Abyssinian, all of which derive from the African wildcat.

Cats are carnivorous animals, agile, with sheathed claws, sharp canine teeth and a keen sense of smell and hearing. Capable of seeing well in the dark, they hunt at night, having learnt their hunting techniques through play.

3 Crack three eggs and put the yolks and whites into a bowl. Whisk thoroughly, adding a little pepper and salt. Melt a little olive oil or butter over a brisk heat in an omelette or small frying pan, tilting the pan to spread the fat. When the oil or butter is hot, pour the whisked eggs carefully into the pan, shifting it backwards and forwards over the heat. Using a spatula, draw the mixture in from the sides of the pan as it cooks and, when it is thick and creamy, spread the mixture evenly over the surface of the pan. After letting the mixture set a little, tilt the pan away from you and fold the omelette into three. Turn the omelette into a pre-heated dish. Garnish with herbs and serve immediately.

5 Common errors

5.1 Singular and plural agreement:

1 (a) the number is   (b) programme is   (c) police are   (d) the chairman was   (e) one leaves
(f) lie traces   (g) a series was

2 Draughts is … darts is (correct) … Each is dealt … a sequence is produced … those aces … . There are two … this pack contains … Someone is cheating … one of my cards is (correct) … those joke packs

3 emerges … every one has … glow … moves … knows … whether these kinds of creatures are

5.2 Mind your verbs:

1 (a) taken   (b) must have   (c) were sitting   (d) overflowed   (e) correct

2 (a) he had made   (b) she had to lie down   (c) he had   (d) said he was
(e) should have … you wrote (or have written)

3 (a) leant   (b) chose   (c) drunk   (d) lay   (e) lying   (f) sown   (g) written   (h) rung   (i) led
(j) flowed

4 Standing lying They had lain looked leant panicked jumped swam

5.3 Comparatives and double negatives:

1 (a) further   (b) more interesting   (c) as powerful as   (d) the eldest of three   (e) less costly
(f) fewer than 8   (g) is better

2 (a) Nobody did anything   (b) He could hardly … the better behaved
(c) didn't know any (or knew none)   (d) You don't know anything (or know nothing) yet.
(e) was trickier (or more tricky)   (f) is worse

3 (a) the better of the two   (b) fewer thrills   (c) is as exciting as if not more exciting than
(d) most remarkable/impressive etc. film … never seen anything (or I've seen nothing)

5.4 All in a twist:

1 (a) only last week   (b) delete one of the "froms"   (c) first three   (d) won both
(e) court before/when   (f) and the 200   (g) different from (or to)

2 reason is that … bored with … preferred to … cough which/that I told you of … fed up with … smoking and

3 which comprises a (or consists of a) … cause of this is that … equally ineffective … different from … boiler nor … recommend either

5.5 Twenty accident blackspots:

1 These are correct: (a) Who's that? It's Jane. And whose car … It's hers … its bumper … know who's done it … it's no business

© Michael Temple: Homework English   Answers

(b) They're not sure ... it's theirs ... but there's no doubt it's not ours. They're off ... but we're staying where we always were.   (c) It's in a class of its own.

2 (a) should have known ... to have knocked ... cup off   (b) Let's see whether we've passed
(c) parking allowed. Be quite quiet   (d) you're not too sure whether   (e) had laid ... had been lying
(f) I'll accept ... except that one   (g) just passed was theirs   (h) were too busy to attend
(i) must have gone past   (j) You're off ... your holidays

3 (a) More people have passed their exams in the past few years.   (b) so loose that I'll lose it.
(c) My principal concern ... a matter of principle   (d) The effect of the ... she was affected by
(e) The building site ... hardly a sight for   (f) Practice makes   (g) know whether the weather will be good   (h) I knew ... a new coat but didn't know

6 Vocabulary skills

6.1 Using a dictionary and thesaurus:
1 (a) changes   (b) skill   (c) impressive   (d) distinguished   (e) miserable
(f) hidden (or underwater)
2 (a) totter   (b) lurch/stagger/totter   (c) trudge   (d) sidle   (e) stagger/totter/lurch   (f) amble   (g) strut
(h) march
3 bang flash round shock utter shrivelled receded immense struck
4 oodles of, lots of, plenty of, a considerable amount of; nicking, stealing, theft, purloining; really chuffed, over the moon, extremely pleased, delighted; pissed, drunk, intoxicated, inebriated

6.2 Express yourself better
1 On the morning of my first day at school I got up and dressed while my mother prepared the breakfast. After that I picked up my pen and pencil and took my cap from the hook. With the aid of a map Dad had already familiarised himself with the route to school, but once in the car we soon found ourselves in a traffic jam and it was obvious we would be lucky to reach school on time. On our eventual arrival I received a nasty shock. There was no one there – we had mistaken the day.
2 a clever/brilliant idea; fine/lovely, pleasant weather; of honest/upright/reliable character; an accurate shot; a convincing performance; a tasty/delicious meal; an enthralling/interesting film
3 (b) To think and write clearly we must try to avoid clichés even though this may be (very) difficult ...
4 soon, now, early, have, thought, if, because
5 (a) It was raining (leave out "literally") cats and dogs   (b) a unique (leave out "quite") ...
(c) The result (leave out "end")
6 If your son fails to attend cricket practice he may not be selected for the team.

6.3 Using imagery:
1 (a) snarled   (b) lays his icy hand   (c) a lion among men ... nerves of steel   (d) tiger   (e) wormed
2 metaphors: crawled, touched, scrambled. The squirrel leapt, wings of the wind, clung, eating, laid hold, gnaw, crept, fledged; similes: like a bright squirrel; as a jaguar creeps on its belly

6.4 Polish your style:
7 cheap, lavatory, large/outsize, bin-man, rubbish dump
8 (a) It suggests that Julian was promoted quickly because his father was chairman of the firm.
(b) It suggests that Mr Smith is the criminal.

Answers

Index

Abbreviations 14
Active and passive 8
Adjectival clauses 40, 42
Adjectives 4
Adverb clauses 40, 42
Adverbs – defined 4
   – spelling 32
Agreement, singular and plural 46
Alliteration 62
Amount and number 50
Apostrophes 18
Articles, definite and indefinite 4
Assonance 62
Balance 62, 52
Base words 30
Brackets 16

Capital letters 12
Clauses – defined, types 40, 42
   – connectors 42, 10
Clichés 58
Climax 62
Collective nouns 46
Colons 22
Commas 16
Common errors 6, 10, 46–54, 58
Comparative and superlative 50
Confused words 50, 54
Conjunctions – 4, 10, 40, 42
   – *so, and, then* 10
Connectors 40, 42
Contractions 14, 18
Contrast 62
Conversation – punctuation 20, 34

Dash 22
Dashes 16
Dependent clauses 40, 42
Dictionary 24, 56
Dots 22
Double negatives 50

Endings 26, 30, 32
Euphemisms 62
Exaggeration 62
Exclamation mark 14

Few, fewer and less 50
Full stop 14, 34

Hyperbole (or exaggeration) 62
Hyphen 22

Imagery 60
Infinitive 8
Informal expressions 58
Innuendo 62
Interjections 4
Inverted commas 20
It's and its 18, 54

Less and few, fewer 50
Lie and lay 48, 54

Metaphors 60

Nouns – defined 4
   – agreement of verb 46
   – proper nouns 4, 12
   – collective nouns 46
   – noun clauses 42
Number and amount 50

Object (and subject) 6, 8
Of, off and have 48, 54
One word or more? 28
Only 52
Onomatopeia 62
Overworked words 58, 10

Paradox 62
Paragraphs – building 44
   – in speech 20
Participial phrases 8
Participles 8
Parts of speech 4
Passed and past 54
Personification 60
Phrases – types 36
   – hanging 38
   – wrongly attached or placed 38
Plural and singular 46
Plurals 32

© Michael Temple: Homework English

Possessive apostrophes 18
Prefixes 30
Prepositions – defined 4
   – problems 6, 52
Pronouns – defined 4
   – problems 6
Proper nouns 4, 12
Punctuation 12–22
Puns 62

Relative pronouns 6, 42
Repetition 58
Rhetorical questions 62
Roots 30

Question mark 14
Quotation marks 20

Semi-colons 22
Sentence 14, 34
Similes 60
Singular and plural 46
Sitting and sat 48
Speech and punctuation 20, 34
Spelling – strategies 24
   – rules 26, 30, 32
   – pronunciation differences 28
   – word-building 30
   – endings 32
Standing and stood 48
Subject – and object 6, 8
   – verb agreement, 6, 46
Suffixes 26, 30, 32
Superlative and comparative 50

Tenses – defined 8
   – *problems* 48
Their, there, they're 54
Thesaurus 56
This, that; these, those 46
Titles 12, 20
Transitive and intransitive 8

Understatement 62

Verbs – defined 4
   – types and forms 8
   – agreement with subject 46
   – problems 46, 48
Vocabulary 56, 58

Who, which, that 6
Who's, whose 54
Wordiness 58
Words often confused 48, 54

Index